"Just as the ruined landscap dreams of the past, so any futi loveliness must first come into the primordial depths within our efforts at purifying this tc mode of presence on the Earth will succeed. The dream not only drives the action, it also guides the action. Through John Perkins's narrative we learn this truth as it is taught with special vividness by the indigenous peoples of South America. Through them we are awakened once again to the wisdom we have forgotten for these many centuries."

—Thomas Berry, author of *The Dream of the Earth* and *The Universe Story* (with Brian Swimme)

"John Perkins is a gifted writer and blessed by the Great Spirit with extraordinary sensitivity and eloquence. This is a moving book of healing and belief in what people of the North usually think of as unbelievable."

—Ipupiara (Bernardo Peixoto), Urueu-Wau-Wau tribe; Ph.D. anthropologist, University of Para, Brazil; advisor to Amazonian Exhibit, Smithsonian Institution.

"A book of stunning power. Every page contains a lesson to be learned and love to be shared."

—Cley Jenny Toscano, Peruvian Quechua healer; anthropologist; lecturer, San Marcos University, Peru, and American University, Washington, D.C.

"John Perkins has lived, listened, talked, and flown with these extraordinary shamans. Now he takes us with him so we can heal the body of our souls and the dreams of the earth."

—Gary Margolis, Ph.D., psychologist; author of *Falling Awake;* director for Counseling/Human Relations, Middlebury College

THE WORLD
IS AS YOU
DREAM IT

SHAMANIC
TEACHINGS
FROM THE
AMAZON
AND ANDES

JOHN PERKINS

Destiny Books
Rochester, Vermont

Destiny Books
One Park Street
Rochester, Vermont 05767

Library of Congress Cataloging-in-Publication Data

Perkins, John M.
    The world is as you dream it : shamanic teachings from the Amazon and Andes / John Perkins.
        p.   cm.
    Includes bibliographical references and index.
    ISBN 0-89281-459-4
    1. Shuar Indians—Religion and mythology. 2. Shuar Indians—Philosophy. 3. Shuar Indians—Drug use. 4. Shamanism—Ecuador. 5. Hallucinogenic drugs and religious experience—Ecuador. 6. Rain forest ecology—Ecuador—Religious aspects. I. Title.
F3722.1.J5P47   1994
299'.883—dc20   93-39493
                                        CIP

Printed and bound in the United States

10 9 8 7 6 5 4 3 2 1

Text design by Charlotte Tyler

Destiny Books is a division of Inner Traditions International

Distributed to the book trade in the United States by American International Distribution Corporation (AIDC)

Distributed to the book trade in Canada by Publishers Group West (PGW), Montreal West, Quebec

Distributed to the book trade in the United Kingdom by Deep Books, London

Distributed to the book trade in Australia by Millennium Books, Newtown, N.S.W.

To Nase, the wind that travels through the forest

blowing balance into all things

Contents

Author's Note   ix
Prologue   xi

Part 1

Quipu Camayoc   3
1. Entering the Dream   6
2. The Shuar   13
3. "Bring People"   30

Part 2

Manco   37
4. Preparation   40
5. Into Ecuador   46
6. Ayahuasca   61
7. A Personal Journey   75

Part 3

The Old Shaman   85
8. The Healing   88
9. Learning from Manco   96
10. Passing On the Dream   107
11. Dream Change   119

Epilogue   122

Glossary   130
Bibliography   136

Author's Note

The events you will read about in the following pages are true. Some, especially those that involve shamanic healings, may stretch the limits of what our northern cultures perceive as credible. In addition to myself, at least five North Americans, including trained medical professionals, witnessed each of the healings and attest to its validity. All the events are re-created as accurately as memory, tape recordings, and scribbled notes permit.

Owing to the sensitive and potentially controversial nature of the material in this book, names and certain other details of people and places have sometimes been changed. This discretion is intended to protect fragile cultures and environments as well as to ensure anonymity.

As a direct result of episodes described in parts 2 and 3, a nonprofit organization known as Earth Dream Alliance (EDA) was established in early 1993. EDA's objective is to transform human consciousness—our collective dream—into a more Earth-honoring one. My workshops and trips to take people to meet the shamans are now conducted in conjunction with EDA. A portion of proceeds from the sale of *The World Is As You Dream It* will be given by the publisher to EDA.

Many people contributed to *The World Is As You Dream It*—men, women, and children who participated in my seminars and workshops, traveled by my side into the Andes and Amazon, and chatted with me on buses or around campfires—you know who you are. You have heard me define *shaman* as one who journeys to other worlds and uses the subconscious, as well as waking reality, in order to effect change. You are shamans to me. The seed for this book was nurtured by our voyages together into those special worlds of friendship, healing, and inspiration. I owe you my eternal gratitude.

My publisher and friend Ehud Sperling traveled with me and encouraged me to reestablish old friendships with the Shuar in the Amazon. Not only has he been a support and kindred spirit to me personally, but he is also, through his business, providing a livelihood and a product that are transforming the lives of many people. I thank him for his love and applaud the example he sets. My thanks go to Estella Arias, whose undying faith in my writing made all of this possible and whose creativity has contributed so much not only to this book but also to the two preceding it. Thanks also to Cornelia Wright, whose editing wizardry brought form out of chaos. They, Leslie Colket, Larry Hamberlin, and others at Inner Traditions are working diligently to change the old materialistic dream into an Earth-honoring one.

I especially thank my family for their commitment and patience throughout all of this, for the journeys they have helped me complete, and for the ones they have taken with me. My mother and father opened the doors, and my wife and daughter continually encourage me to go out and explore new territory. My two Ecuadoran partners—guides, teachers, and mentors—have become brothers to me; their tenderness and strength have pulled me and so many others out of frightening and often dangerous situations. I thank them from the bottom of my heart.

Of course, above all I thank the great shamans. It is you who hold the torches that will light the pathways into the new dream. I am grateful beyond words to you as a group and especially to my individual teachers—men and women who are united in the belief that we can and must change, who honor Mother Earth, and who set inspiring examples for the rest of us to follow. You have sat with me and walked with me; shared your homes, food, and philosophies; and given me and others so much of your time, wisdom, and compassion. *The World Is As You Dream It* is your belief. This is your book.

Prologue

Only now, when the tribal peoples have almost gone, has the West awakened to the fact that, rather than their lands and possessions, it is their subtle abilities and specialized environmental wisdom, forged since the beginning of time, which are of paramount importance to us all. The new psychologies of hypnotic suggestion and "creative visualization" are increasingly aware that we are capable of infinitely more than the assumed constraints of "physical laws" on our bodies and minds would have us believe.

Lawrence Blair, *Ring of Fire*

Miami threatened to explode. The second trial was over. The jury had reached its verdict, but the announcement had been delayed. If the white police officer had been found innocent in the shooting of the black motorcyclist, the city would erupt—a repeat of the violence four years earlier following acquittal in the original trial, except this time the rioting would be even worse. Thousands of people had been homeless for nearly a year as a result of Hurricane Andrew. Thousands more were out of work. They were desperate and angry.

Helicopters circled the city. Sirens screamed. The message was clear: demonstrations would not be tolerated. Television screens were filled with helmeted police officers armed for war.

The university where I was lecturing had fortified itself. It was a liberal institution that offered generous scholarships to children of the poor neighborhoods surrounding its normally tranquil campus. Yet today its regents were terrified of the residents of those neighborhoods. The administration had given me and everyone else inside the university's walls exactly one hour to either get as far away as possible or remain inside. The gates would close at 4:30 P.M., fifteen minutes before the verdict was to be announced.

I was driving north on Interstate 95 toward my home in Palm Beach County. My wife, Winifred, and eleven-year-old daughter, Jessica, had planned to join me for a weekend in Miami. Those plans had now changed.

I pushed the "scan" button on the car radio.

"The Founding Fathers," a voice said, "dreamed of a judicial system based on equality." The scanner moved on. I switched off the radio, impressed by the statement I had just heard. I knew the voice was talking about the trial. Yet it also had spoken prophetically to our entire culture, for like every other society, ours is shaped by the dreaming of its members. I glanced out the window and wondered about my country. What is our dream—now and for future generations? I knew that one way to understand a society's dreams is to analyze its accomplishments. I asked myself, What do we do best?

The course I was teaching at the university was called Philosophy 261; the subject, however, was dreaming. I was teaching about the dreams of individuals—Socrates, Buddha, Christ, Martin Luther King, Jr.—and the dreams of cultures—those of ancient Egypt and Mesopotamia, our own, and especially the contemporary indigenous cultures of the Andes and Amazon. My students were preparing for a month of study with the shamans of South America, people who, like their counterparts in tribal cultures throughout the world, acknowledge the power of dreams and nurture the wisdom of the subconscious. The title *shaman,* used widely today in place of the more restrictive "medicine man" or the pejorative "witch doctor," is bestowed upon men and women who journey into the subconscious, to parallel worlds, or to what the Australian Aborigines refer to as the Dreamtime, in order to heal and effect changes in people and nature. The underlying assumption of Philosophy 261—at least my version of it—was that the shamans possess a knowledge that we in our culture have lost and need to regain.

Every culture on this planet believes in the incredible power of dreams or comes from a heritage that once believed in this power. Many equate dreams with the latent energy of the seed and embryo. Their beliefs are not unlike Carl Jung's theory that humanity's collective unconscious contains the knowledge of all past and future events and that dreams are a key for tapping into this vast library of information.

That morning I had read to my class from Robert Lawlor's remarkable book *Voices of the First Day: Awakening in the Aboriginal Dreamtime:*

> The Australian Aborigines, and indeed indigenous tribal peoples all over the world, believe that the spirit of their consciousness and way of life exists like a seed buried in the earth. The waves of European colonialism that destroyed the civilizations of North America, South America, and Australia began a five-hundred-year dormancy period of the "archaic consciousness." Its potencies disappeared into the earth. . . .

> Dreams, deep collective memories, and imaginings are more potent than religious faith or scientific theories in lifting us above the catastrophic ending that confronts us all.*

Every one of the students had agreed that dreaming is the most powerful thing we do in life. It forms the bases for our perceptions, attitudes, emotions, motivations, and actions. It occurs all the time, at both conscious and subconscious levels: while we are working, driving our cars, preparing food, reading, and watching television—as well as during sleep. Individual dreams affect the courses of our lives; collective dreams determine the futures of civilizations.

I looked through the windshield out onto Interstate 95, at the congested traffic, the crisscrossing overpasses, the vast expanses of asphalt, the concrete buildings that form a nearly continuous stretch of city up the coast of Florida, and thought about a newspaper article one of my students had brought to class. It stated that from 1983 to 1989, 55 percent of all wealth in the United States went to one half of one percent of the population. Again I asked the question, What do we do best?

Then I saw the answer right in front of me, shockingly apparent. The answer to my question was scrawled across the billboards; it flashed from the tops of buildings; it was etched in the surface of the highway. It was going on all around me.

Construction. Remolding the Earth. Bulldozing, mining, and building. We are proficient at these. We pave and roof over with amazing dedication and efficiency. We build sidewalks, roads, highways, cars, trucks, airplanes, houses, skyscrapers, shopping malls, and factories. Through construction, we divert rivers, turn mountains into valleys, irrigate deserts, drain swamps, and control the climates of huge housing complexes. It is what we do best. As I was digesting this thought, I realized that practically everything we do is judged by how well it supports our construction endeavors. Our educational, commercial, political, social, and judicial systems are all set up to enhance the efficiency of construction.

The ramifications of this philosophy reach far beyond our country's borders. Not only have we encouraged others to follow our example through our development programs, but we have also ravaged their natural resources and polluted their environment to feed our greedy lifestyle.

How do we justify this behavior? Those countries that do not measure

---

*Robert Lawlor, *Voices of the First Day: Awakening in the Aboriginal Dreamtime* (Rochester, Vt.: Inner Traditions, 1991), pp. 6, 8.

up to our materialistic standards we label as "underdeveloped." The insult this term inflicts on ancient, proud cultures has been devestating. I remembered an Iranian scholar, Professor Ghazanfari, whom I got to know while working on a World Bank project in his country in 1977. He had pointed out that the words *developed* and *underdeveloped,* first coined in this context by President Truman and probably intended to be compassionate, evoke strong feelings of superiority and inferiority. For a long time we, the "developed," have assumed the patronizing attitude that while other countries should adopt our values, their cultures have little to offer us—except oil, timber, gold, and other natural resources.

The environmental destruction this mind-set has brought is well known. But equally damaging is the attitude behind labeling two thirds of the world as "underdeveloped." By categorizing indigenous cultures of the "Third World" according to their lack of industrial wealth and ignoring or denigrating the dreams that enable them to live in harmony with their environment, "First World" countries limit their own dream perception, in effect trapping themselves and others in a cycle of destruction.

Professor Ghazanfari had reinforced an idea that had been growing in me during my decade-long career as a consultant to international development agencies, the idea that perception is the single most important factor in shaping the future. In Java and Egypt, Sulawesi and Mexico, I witnessed time and again the power certain individuals have in altering perceptions and, in so doing, changing people's lives. These individuals took many forms: tribal chieftains, magicians, dancers, Dalang puppet masters, priests, firewalkers, politicians, and healers. In my own country, the most influential wore business suits, read the *Wall Street Journal,* and invested billions of dollars each year in advertising. Whatever their appearance or title, they all had one thing in common: their power came from their ability to mold dreams.

A road sign informed me that I had left Dade County and the threat of mass violence behind. I felt relieved. Then a picture of armed police officers preparing for a riot flashed before me. Even if downtown Miami were vacated, if the university were totally emptied of people, those officers would still be there to defend the buildings. It was the construction and the materialistic dream it represents, more than the human beings, that was being protected. But who benefits from that dream?

Most people throughout the ages would view modern "construction" as a horrible sacrilege; they would condemn it as an act of violence against God and Earth, as the systematic and wanton "destruction" of the very forces we depend on for life. The sad fact is that the material wealth generated by the concrete cities and asphalt highways benefits a very small percentage of just one of Earth's thirty million or so species. The rest of us must suffer the consequences of vanishing forests, polluted air, poisoned water, and loss of biodiversity. Statistics concerning divorce, suicide, and other indicators of personal unhappiness leave us wondering whether even those few in that small percentile are really benefiting.

Off in the distance I spied the stacks of one of Florida Power and Light Company's plants. I thought about the many years I had devoted to promoting construction, first as a consultant to the World Bank and the United Nations, and later as owner and CEO of a company that developed, owned, and operated power plants. I had followed the short-sighted leaders of our culture, "experts" who, like shamans, had molded our dreams. Moreover, I realized, I had become one of those false shamans.

I had accepted the philosophy that had shaped most of my post–World War II culture: happiness is a new bike, a bigger car, or a more expensive house in the suburbs. I bought into the dream of business school. I tried desperately to claw my way into that tiny percentile at the top of the economic ladder. Now, as I prepared to take a group of university students to work with the Earth-honoring shamans of South America, I wondered why I had allowed myself to be persuaded to deviate so far from the beliefs of my childhood.

As infants we enjoy an intimacy with everything around us: tiny stones, butterflies, flowers, birds, animals both stuffed and real. We live in a world of beauty and imagination. Ecstasy comes easily. We feel at one with nature and the realm of dreams.

Growing into childhood, we begin to understand the power of the dream, of fairy tales and myths; we know that dreams come true and that many different parallel worlds exist simultaneously. The past, the future, the present: these are meaningless to us, for we have the ability to blend them into one. We can be anything we want at any time. All we have to do is dream it and it will happen. We can drift into another world and out again whenever we so desire.

Then at some point in our lives, that awareness changes. Adults convince us that we are not all one. They teach us how to separate and alienate ourselves from one another and from the world around us. To describe our parallel worlds, they spit out phrases such as "unhealthy daydreaming" and "crazy flights of fantasy" as though the very words threaten to contaminate their lips. They warn us that to continue in our old ways will be immature and impractical.

My childhood dreams were shaped by places I knew intimately: forests, rivers, and lakes with Indian names that surrounded the New Hampshire village where I grew up. I dreamed of visiting my pioneering ancestors and the Indian neighbors they fought and sometimes loved.

My grandfather used to sit in a weathered rocking chair next to his potbellied stove and regale me with tales about his adventurous youth. As a child, he had traveled with his parents in a covered wagon on the long march from New Hampshire to the Dakotas. They had built a homestead not far from the place white people call the Little Bighorn.

"Indians!" Grandpa would shout, whacking the arm of his chair. "I'll say I've seen plenty!" One day he pointed proudly at his angular nose and told me that his profile was the result of a liaison between his great-grandmother and an Abnaki chief—a statement adamantly rejected by my parents, for in those days having indigenous blood was not considered something to brag about.

My parents used to take me every summer to Fort Ticonderoga in upstate New York. As we wandered through the museum and along ancient stone corridors, they tried valiantly to draw my attention to the Revolutionary War heroism of Ethan Allen, a distant relative on my father's side; but my imagination carried me back to the earlier French and Indian War, to Indians who won battles by using their knowledge of nature to outsmart European invaders, and to white men who learned from native shamans.

As I grew older, I spent more time in the forests. An only child, I took solace in the Iroquois philosophy that plants and animals are our brothers and sisters. After school I frequently visited an old hermit who lived in the woods and claimed to be half Abnaki.

One evening as I was falling asleep, my mother came into my room. "I know about your dream," she said. "But you must put it aside now. The frontier is gone." She sat on the bed next to me and spoke in her gentlest voice. "There are no more Indians, Johnny, at least not like the ones in your books. Perhaps your dad and I have been wrong to encourage your imagination." She stroked my face, and I sensed that she didn't entirely believe what she said. She sighed. "But anyway, the idea is still there." She seemed to search. "The ideal. You know, old and true values." She patted my hand. "There's another ancestor in your background you might like to know. Your fifth great-grandfather was an idea man. He may help you redirect your energies." She set a book, Thomas Paine's *Common Sense,* down on my bedside table.

Common Sense forever changed my life. It taught me the power of words. By the time I reached junior high I had learned to combine my interest in nature and Indian lore with writing. For a seventh-grade history project, I finished a novel I had begun writing the previous summer. Entitled "Trail to the North," it was the story of a band of Abnakis who desperately tried to stop the encroaching Europeanization of the Connecticut River Valley by sweeping south from present-day Canada to raid isolated farms. They took captives back to their village in the hope that by teaching them Indian ways they could change the course of history.

My teacher, Mrs. Simpson, asked me to remain after school one day. Terrified, I sat in a chair beside her desk. She handed me "Trail to the North." I scanned the cover, where I had drawn a bark longhouse in a forest clearing. No grade. A knot began to tighten in my stomach until I opened my novel to the first page and found a tiny A. When I looked up, unable to suppress my joy, Mrs. Simpson handed me a large book. There before me was a photograph of an Indian longhouse in a clearing, remarkably similar to the one on the cover of my manuscript. From the angle I could tell that the photographer had been in an airplane. Then my heart gave a leap. A man, naked except for a feathered headband and loincloth, stood in a shadow next to the house; his left hand held a bow, and his right had drawn the bowstring all the way back to his jaw. The arrow was aimed up, through the camera lens, directly at me. I knew that somehow I was part of that picture.

I felt Mrs. Simpson's eyes on me. "Yes," she said. "That photograph was taken in the Amazon rain forest last year. People still live like your Abnakis." She reached out and, in a highly unusual gesture, touched my arm. "Dreams do come true, you know."

Interstate 95, as it passed beneath my car, reminded me of a highway described in a book that had influenced me at another critical turning point in my life. During the late 1970s and early 1980s I had become disturbed by the World Bank's insensitivity to environmental issues. After much soul-searching, I decided to give up a lucrative and prestigious career. Deep in my heart I wanted to start my own company, one that would help the environment, but I wavered. It was a big plunge, fraught with risk.

A friend handed me a book by a native North American shaman, John Fire Lame Deer. One particular passage so impressed me that now, a decade later, I continue to read it to my classes. Lame Deer describes the people of modern cultures as follows:

> They have forgotten the secret knowledge of their bodies, their senses, or their dreams. They don't use the knowledge the spirit has put into every one of them; they are not even aware of this, and so they stumble along blindly on the road to nowhere—a paved highway which they themselves bulldoze and make smooth so that they can get faster to the big, empty hole which they'll find at the end, waiting to swallow them up.*

My interest in Lame Deer was part of a quest to learn more about this secret knowledge, shamanism. Although I had met many shamans during my Peace Corps work in the Amazon and the Andes from 1968 to 1971,

---

*John Fire Lame Deer and Richard Erdoes, *Lame Deer, Sioux Medicine Man*, (London: Quartet, 1980), p. 157.

and as an international development consultant in the 1970s, it was Lame
Deer who inspired me to dig deep into the ancient chronicles and modern
texts on the subject. I discovered that people with impeccable credentials,
such as Mircea Eliade, chairman of the Department of History of Religions
at the University of Chicago and author of *Shamanism: Archaic Techniques
of Ecstasy*, took shamanism very seriously. I also discovered that many of
the great figures of history were by definition shamans: Plato, Socrates,
Zoroaster, Moses, Ezekiel, Muhammed, Buddha, Christ, Galileo, Mozart,
Edison, and so many others were people who used the power of the subconscious to bring about change.

The books I read described cultures where miracles are part of everyday life, where people wear feathers to help them fly into the sky above
and turtle shells to enable them to visit the worlds below. These were serious books by academics, physicists, and medical doctors. I found that my
boyhood dream about learning from indigenous teachers was not only
coming to life but was also coming together with other people's dreams.

The secret knowledge described by Lame Deer is no secret to most of
the people we disdainfully refer to as "primitive." Throughout the world,
these people understand the power of dreams—the images, voices, smells,
feelings, and tastes that inhabit the inner recesses of the body and soul. They
realize that dreaming is not restricted to the hours when we sleep and that
when we honor our dreams we empower ourselves. They have developed
highly successful techniques for tapping into "the knowledge that the spirit
has put into everyone." They have come to know that all power, dreams,
energy, balance, and health originate in the Earth, and that if we are to
survive as a species we must set as our highest priority the preservation of
Earth herself.

Intellectually I understood this. Lame Deer inspired me to experience
it. I began to open my senses to the spirits within. It took practice and patience, but slowly I progressed. I opened my heart to the world around me
and did what every elementary school student in our culture is discouraged
from doing: I daydreamed. And nightdreamed. I allowed the messages of
my subconscious to surface. I examined them from every angle, and little
by little I started to follow the suggestions they gave me.

It worked. At first I used this knowledge solely to help myself, primarily to manage the stresses I encountered in running a multimillion-dollar
company. My experiences resulted in a book: *The Stress-Free Habit: Powerful Techniques for Health and Longevity from the Andes, Yucatan, and
Far East.*

Increasingly, however, I became aware of the larger implications. I recognized that we all constantly make choices that affect our cultures in profound and lasting ways and that our collective choice to ignore the "knowl-

edge of the spirit" is doing exactly what Lame Deer predicted: taking us "blindly on the road to nowhere," into that empty hole at the end. I began to develop an approach that would offer alternatives. This work resulted in another book, one with a less self-centered, more social and global theme: *Psychonavigation: Techniques for Travel beyond Time.*

The two books were well received. They brought me invitations to speak to large audiences—and excuses to spend more time with people in Ecuador I had first met twenty-five years earlier during my tour with the Peace Corps. I was asked to take several groups of psychologists, doctors, and other medical professionals to study with Amazonian and Andean shamans, as described later in this book.

One evening I was sitting on the dirt floor of a shaman's lodge deep in the Amazon rain forest. The shaman—a former headhunter and respected elder of the Shuar tribe—was chanting into the embers of a sacred fire. Seated in a circle around the fire were eight U.S. psychotherapists. During a mere six days in this land, each of them had developed a deep respect for the spiritual powers, environmental wisdom, and healing skills of the shamans. I recalled my childhood dream. The French and Indian War was long over, yet here were white people who were learning from Indian shamans. They would return to their world forever changed. The lessons and wisdom of nature were being passed on again.

The World Is As You Dream It, though different from *The Stress-Free Habit* and *Psychonavigation,* is, I believe, part of a progression. For me, the first step was to become more self-aware and centered, more stress-free. Next came the recognition that my decisions affect everything around me, and that through psychonavigation I could gain insight into my own role as an Earth steward, as well as an individual, businessman, husband, and father.

This third book is about a social movement. It is about U.S. medical doctors, businesspeople, teachers, students, housewives, and others from the industrial North. It is about tribal elders, shamans, herbal healers, and others from the South. It is about people throughout the world who are recognizing the need for profound change. On one level, it tells the stories of individuals from extremely diverse cultures who have reached a similar conclusion: that in order for life to continue as we know it, we must all change our dream from the one of materialism and domination that has ruled supreme for so long to a more spiritual, cooperative, and Earth-honoring one. It describes the coming together of these people from such different—and seemingly irreconcilable—backgrounds and the sharing that has resulted, the exchange of wisdom, the compassion, inspiration, and the commitments to follow through on changing the dream. On another level, it provides a road map that every reader can follow in order to distinguish dreams from fantasies and make the dreams come true.

It is also the story of my own personal development and of the Ecuadoran teachers who guided me, for only by telling that small story can I raise the curtain to the larger one. If the smaller at times gets in the way of the larger, I apologize and ask that you look beyond it. I believe that by doing so, you will see that *The World Is As You Dream It* is also your story, an adventure that will take you into new and wonderfully beautiful worlds.

For most of us the power of dreams is snatched away during an educational process that focuses on the material world. The shamans you will meet in this book were educated very differently. They have a great deal to teach us. It is important to keep in mind, however, that you do not have to visit these shamans personally in order to empower yourself and make your own dreams come true. The knowledge is within you; it was there at birth and stayed with you through much of your childhood. If you fear you have lost it, turn that fear around. Think of it as knowledge that went underground for a while. Lame Deer emphasizes that "the spirit" put this wisdom into everyone, but many in our culture have forgotten it. What we forget we can also remember.

The stories in this book, the examples of the indigenous peoples of the Andes and the Amazon, and the shamanic journeys and teachings are here to help stimulate your memory and subconscious visions. They are here to open doors and push the walls of your understanding to the horizon.

The challenge, then, is to combine what we have learned through our contemporary education about the material world with what we know deep in our hearts about the subconscious and parallel worlds—in ways that will provide a beautiful future for the children of all species. The world is indeed as we dream it.

Part ❀ One

Quipu Camayoc

Dawn arrived quickly, as it always does in the Andes. The first specks of silver were followed immediately by streaks of orange and magenta along the mountaintops. The young runner stood alone beside the ancient road and watched Inti, the sun, rise to greet him. Every morning brought another miracle of light and warmth, but this dawn was unlike any other.

Manco would become the latest member of his family to enter the proud ranks of the quipu camayocs. Since long before the Spaniards had come to impose their will on the world, the quipu camayocs had been keepers of records, teachers, the people who, through their disciplined system of relay runners, had kept all four corners of the vast Incan Empire united.

Manco straightened. He turned his head, eager to catch the sound of an approaching runner. He would hear the other's footsteps on the far side of the hill before seeing the head and shoulders as he climbed the steep dirt road. Manco had seen it in his mind many times. He returned his attention to Inti and bowed solemnly.

Then a breath caught in his throat. He strained to hear. Involuntarily he gave a little leap. There was no mistaking the rhythm of the other runner's feet on the hard-packed dirt. Manco took a deep breath and let it out slowly. He removed his poncho, folded it, held it out toward the rising sun, and set it gently at the side of the road. He thanked Inti for the honor bestowed on him and prayed that he would do his part without faltering.

A head came over the hill. It shimmered phantomlike in the morning mist. Manco blew his conch shell. The head rose. The runner picked up speed. Manco reviewed the sprint ahead in his mind one last time.

As the final *quipu camayoc*, Manco would cover only a short distance. But he must do it quickly and with dignity. He bent his front knee slightly, extended his left hand as far behind as he could reach, and concentrated on the sounds of the other's approach.

The runner's breathing was hard but steady, his footfalls in perfect rhythm, like the shaman's drum. Manco knew he must be exhausted, but the runner had been trained in the Condor Way and was now looking down on the road through the condor's eyes high above. His dream had joined the dream of the Universal Spirit.

Suddenly Manco's hand felt the leather pouch. His fingers closed around it. He heard the condor's scream burst from his throat as he leapt high into the air.

He skimmed across the surface of the road. The wind cooled and sang to him. There came a throbbing, the rhythm of his wings. The sun reached fingers of energy out to him. He felt euphoric. He looked down and saw the land beneath, then his village.

Before Manco knew what had happened, an elder, Sinchi, appeared. He was waving the sacred *huaca* staff. Manco flew to him, vaguely aware that a throng of villagers cheered him on. He handed the precious pouch to Sinchi. Someone wrapped a poncho around Manco's shoulders and helped him inside the house.

The interior was uncharacteristically light. A row of candles encircled the cot where Manco's pregnant mother lay. Her eyes met his; they were full of pride in the knowledge that her first child was now a *quipu camayoc*. When Sinchi reached the center of the room, he held the pouch up to the ceiling and the sky above. He offered it to each of the four corners of the universe. Finally he set it down on the dirt floor and kneeled next to it. Chanting softly to the Earth, he emptied the contents into his hand—a pile of golden corn seeds. His voice grew louder.

"The seed is the dream of life," he chanted. "The seed is past and future spirit." He rose and slowly lifted the hand to his mouth. "The seed dreams itself into a tall stalk that bears the sacred fruit." He sucked in his breath and placed the now-empty hand against his heart.

Sinchi took his *huaca* staff and went to Manco's mother, pulling back the alpaca blanket, exposing the mountainous bare *stomach. The woman looked up and smiled that gentle smile that always warmed Manco to the bottom of his soul. The elder bent low over her and made a hissing noise. When he stepped back, the seeds circled her navel.*

"The seed and womb dream themselves," Sinchi chanted. "Each dreams the other." He bowed to the four corners. "The seed dreams of being eaten. The baby dreams of corn in her stomach." He returned to the woman. Again he bent down. This time he kissed her womb. The corn disappeared.

Huaca staff in hand, Sinchi walked slowly out the door. Manco grabbed the stick that had been his grandfather's and his father's before him and followed. He was relieved to see that the sky was cloudless. Inti was not even tempted to hide himself from this ceremony. The villagers followed them into the field. The Elder repeated his chant and slowly, one by one, spit the corn seeds into Pachamama, Mother Earth. With his stick, Manco tamped each deep into its own womb and prayed to the gods that the dream of the seeds would be realized.

1

Entering the Dream

My conversation with Mrs. Simpson about "Trail to the North" encouraged me to see the world with new eyes. A few years later, in high school, I dreamed of being a writer and influencing people. I hoped that someday I could convey the Abnaki message—through words instead of violence.

The image of the Amazonian man in Mrs. Simpson's photo haunted me. I wanted to meet him. I was certain that I needed experience much more than college. But back in the sixties, if you were poor, had good grades, and received a scholarship, you went to college. My father would not listen to pleas that I could pursue a writing career by joining the Merchant Marine or going to work for a big city newspaper. He had sacrificed all his life, he told me, so I could have things he had only dreamed about. Defeated, I went to Middlebury College, my mother's alma mater.

Despite its charms, I disliked Middlebury from the start. I had no use for the way my Freshman English professor eruditely analyzed poetry as though it should follow rules like those of algebra. I resented the snobbish attitude of the rich kids there (Middlebury then boasted the highest percentage of students listed on the New York *Social Register* of any college in the country) and loathed their Porsches and Jaguars. Most of all I hated the location. The forests had been replaced by fields. The town lacked the attractions of a city and yet had none of the backwoods rough-and-tumble atmosphere I had grown up with in New Hampshire. I felt terribly alone and despondent. Every chance I got, I traveled to Boston to visit Mary, a girl I had dated during our senior year in high school. Her grades had not been very good, and she had had the courage to shun college in order to pursue the glamour, money, and free-wheeling lifestyle of a modeling career. She was a beautiful eagle, soaring; I was a caged canary.

In Boston I felt liberated. For the first time in my life I ventured on my own to museums and theaters, browsed in bookstores, and reveled in the parade of people from all walks of life and from all parts of the world that passed before me. I also spent a lot of time waiting for Mary to finish up a fashion show or photo shoot. My favorite place was a little café that served cheap draft beer; behind the bar hanging on the wall was a fanciful tapestry that never failed to take me to a distant and unknown land. A placard next to it explained that it had been made by the Huichol Indians of the Sierra Madre in Central Mexico.

The tapestry showed mountains, corn, mythical birds, a rainbow, and the sun, all in vibrant colors and all seemingly interconnected by waxy strings. Since beginning my studies at Middlebury, I had dreamed recurrently about an Indian boy named Manco running through high mountains; the dream images had included a gigantic bird, corn, and a glaring sun. Whenever I looked at the tapestry, I remembered the dream, as though the two were somehow related.

One afternoon, an elderly gentleman sat down next to me. When I finished my beer he ordered me another. Then he introduced himself. The tapestry was his. It had been given to him by a Huichol friend, a fact that impressed me greatly. Not since that afternoon with Mrs. Simpson had it occurred to me that modern human beings—U.S. citizens like this man sitting at the bar beside me—were actually in contact with Indians, close enough contact to be honored with gifts as precious as this tapestry.

"The Huichol are a remarkable people," he said. "They still maintain customs that predate Columbus." He explained that every year the Huichol are led on a pilgrimage by powerful shamans to a place called Wirikuta. In so doing, they retrace the steps of their ancestors, the Ancient Ones, who through their wanderings wove together the elements of the world: all the plants, animals, stones, mountains, rivers, and oceans. He pointed at the tapestry. "The Huichol believe that we are all one with each other, all part of the great cosmic dream. They express this in their art."

At the end of his discourse, his eyes met mine. "I've seen you sitting here studying that tapestry before," he said. "I couldn't help but notice how unhappy you look."

In those days I was not a particularly open person, yet for some reason I told this stranger about my dislike of Middlebury. I told him that I had always dreamed of traveling, living with Indians, and writing.

"Then that is your journey to Wirikuta," he said, smiling kindly. "It is a sacred covenent you must keep with yourself." He lifted his mug and touched mine. "Never mind what your father says. You must listen to your heart. It speaks to you from a place of great wisdom. That is why you always return here to stare at that tapestry. You may travel your own route, but to Wirikuta you must go." I felt a huge weight lift from my shoulders.

The next day I spent several hours in the Boston Public Library. I learned that what he had told me about the Huichol was indeed true, and that their belief in a cosmic unity—a sort of empathetic pact between all things—has much in common with the beliefs of many other peoples throughout the world: the Shuar and other Amazonian tribes, the Quechua of the Andes, the Maya of Central America, the Badyaranke of Senegal, the Bugis of Indonesia, the Polynesians and Hawaiians, and many North American and Eskimo groups. By the time I walked out into the sunlight of Copley Square my head was reeling. Euphoric, I knew that I had only touched the surface of something vast, something that reached deep inside and tugged at the roots of my subconscious. I had also made up my mind.

Ten days later, I quit Middlebury College and landed a job in Boston as a copyboy for the Boston *Record American*. I soared like an eagle. That pivotal decision taught me more about myself than anything I had ever done before.

Leaving Middlebury began to open a door for me, a door that helped me acknowledge something I had known as a child: our dreams have a way of turning into reality.

Children enjoy a feeling of unity with everything in their lives; they see themselves as not "separate from" but rather "part of." When I was a child I could become anything or anyone I wanted to be—a tree, Peter Pan, an Indian chief. All I had to do was dream it and believe it. Like the Huichol in Wirikuta, I was one with all, part of the cosmic dream.

Then adults taught me and my friends to believe that we were *not* one, to segregate things, to categorize and break them down into their smallest components. Our favorite stories, we were told, were "kid stuff" with no relevance in the adult world. Daydreaming was discouraged, even punished. Nightdreaming became a game to be deciphered by a book with cute little descriptions that ignored the incredible power dreams possess. We knew the terror of nightmares and the ecstasy of prepuberty dreams, but we were told to shrug these off. Some of us were severely chastised when we discussed them. It did not take long for us to learn.

The Huichol, on the other hand, encourage the dreaming process throughout life. They use their incredible tapestries and their annual pilgrimages to Wirikuta to celebrate and formalize the entry into these parallel worlds. Like other cultures—cultures each of us can trace our heritage back to—the Huichol also use the plant kingdom as a teacher. But I knew nothing of that the day I left Middlebury.

The Boston *Record American* was one of the last of the old Hearst tabloids, specializing in crime, political scandals, and sports. Its reporters reflected the newspaper's personality: they dressed flamboyantly, chewed on stubby cigars, and sauntered about the city room as though they owned the world.

I loved my job. The city room, where I worked, was the heart of the newspaper. The smell of cigar smoke and newsprint was intoxicating. Overheard conversations about Mafia bosses fired my imagination. The excitement of the place was beyond my wildest expectations: reporters dashed in and out, phones rang ceaselessly, and eccentric characters loitered about, waiting to be interviewed.

My days as a copyboy were threatened when President Johnson sent more troops to Vietnam. The only way for me to keep my job and avoid the draft was to return to college. Middlebury was out of the question. Reluctantly, I enrolled in Boston University.

In the sixties Boston's colleges, like those throughout the nation, were preoccupied with Vietnam, drugs, and sex. *Record American* readers loved to read about all three. This created a rare opportunity for me. Under ordinary circumstances, I would have had to serve an apprenticeship for a least two years before even thinking about becoming a reporter. Circumstances, however, were far from ordinary.

I wrote a short article for the Sunday edition about the sexual revolution; nothing very provocative, it focused on young unmarrieds who were living together. That article was followed by interviews with students who either supported or opposed the Johnson administration's Vietnam policies. I felt comfortable with both issues, since I could relate to them personally. But my next assignment, on hallucinogenic drugs, terrified me. I had never tried any drugs, not even the ubiquitous marijuana, and was frightened by the prospect of even interviewing people involved in such activities.

At the time, Timothy Leary and Richard Alpert were making headlines with the work they were conducting on LSD through Harvard's Center for Personality Research. My editor convinced me that drug research in a college setting would be a safe subject, so with trepidation I called the Department of Ethnobotany at Harvard's Botanical Museum to get the name of someone familiar with psychotropic drugs. Over the phone I was introduced to Bob Gutierrez, a young man who would have a profound effect on my life.

Bob agreed to meet me under an ancient oak tree not far from the entrance to the Botanical Museum. He had sounded rational enough on the phone, but when I saw him approaching, my heart sank. His unkempt appearance and long hair gave me an anxiety attack. He smiled in an innocent yet unnerving way and pointed toward the museum. "The great man's domain," he said, and then led me to a small bench in the shade of the tree. I squeezed myself into a corner of the bench as far away from him as I could get.

After some small talk, I mentioned Leary and Alpert. Bob gave me a strange look. "They're just short-haulers," he hissed, tossing his long hair in a dismissive gesture. "Joyriders who think LSD is Lord Science's gift to university students."

I was amazed and a bit relieved. "And you disagree?"

"You didn't know?" He was unable or unwilling to hide his contempt. "You obviously haven't done your homework." Then he laughed. "I'm a student of Richard Schultes, the ethnobotanist who has turned that place upside down," he said, indicating the museum. "We don't agree with Leary about much." He explained that Schultes had devoted his life to studying rain forest Indians in order to learn about their ways of healing, especially the uses they make of plants. "Of course that includes psychoactive varieties."

"Like LSD?"

His look made me want to crawl under the bench. "LSD is not a plant substance—not of Mother Earth, but rather of Lord Science, a false god. It is taken by uneducated people to escape from the problems of this world. Psychoactive plants are studied for years by tribal shamans and taken in order to become one with the world."

I asked whether he included Dr. Leary among the uneducated.

"Absolutely," he responded with a condescending smile, then proceeded to launch into a dissertation on the evils of our education system, a system, he said, "that forces us to worship Lord Science at the expense of everything else."

He stood up and walked to the trunk of the oak. "This tree alive can teach us far more than the words of experts written on the paper it could produce dead. Amazonian Indians know the power of plants. If one were here right now, he would tell you that this tree possesses the wisdom of the universe, as do all plants." He returned to the bench. "So do we humans. The problem is that we in the 'civilized' world have forgotten how to use the wisdom that is our birthright, part of our DNA."

He sat down and told me the story of Schultes's first experience with ayahuasca, a potent hallucinogen used by Amazonian shamans. "Its name means 'vine of the soul,'" he said, "and it allows the user to return to Mother Earth's womb, the source of all things." He explained that the Indians with whom Schultes worked believe that a person who drinks the juice of a psychoactive plant is able to see that he and the plant share a common origin and thus are inseparably united. "The evolutionist's idea that life is a pyramid with man sitting on the top is an absurdity invented by a few manipulative scientists. Perception—it is all a matter of perception. The Indians— like the ancient Greeks, Celts, Egyptians, and everyone else except what we call the 'modern civilized world'—perceive things very differently."

By the time he finished, my anxiety had dissipated. I could not help but be impressed by what he said. It was all rather new and foreign to me, and yet it sounded so very . . . the only word I could come up with was *sane*.

"A matter of perception," he repeated. "Who knows where the truth lies, if there is such a thing? But I think we can say this: that our culture's perception is extremely self-centered, greedy, and probably in the final analysis self-destructive. The Indian perception, on the other hand, is nuturing, endurable, self-sustaining." He looked me in the eye. "And theirs is so much more optimistic. When I'm on my deathbed, I'd sure as hell rather believe that I'm about to return to Mother Earth's womb than that I'm going to any of the places civilized religions offer."

Years later, I would study Schultes' extensive writings. By that time he had become the world's preeminent authority on tropical plants. Timothy Leary faded into the background, but Richard Schultes left an indelible mark.

I would learn from Schultes that ayahuasca is also known as *yaje* and *caapi*, and that its scientific name is *Banisteriopsis caapi*. Highly toxic, it belongs to the Malpighiaceae family and contains a group of alkaloids known as beta carbolines, of which harmine is the primary component. Eventually I would watch Amazonian shamans prepare it, often boiling it with other plants. Schultes would tell me that these other plants include chacruna (*Psychotria viridis,* of the Rubiaceae, or coffee, family), chagropanga (*Diplopterys cabrerana,* also of the Malpighiaceae family), chiricaspi (*Brunfelsia chiricaspi*), and chiric-sanango (*Brunfelsia grandiflora,* var. *Schultesii*—named after the man himself). These additives generally contain tryptamines and serve to lengthen and strengthen the effects of the ayahuasca.*

My own experiences, along with what I learned from Schultes and others, would teach me that "vine of the soul" is not a particularly accurate translation of the term used by the shamans, since the concept of soul as we think of it is not applicable in cultures where cosmology is based on the oneness of all things. The shamans who speak Spanish as a second language continue to use this translation, however, along with "vine of spirit wisdom" and "vine of death."

Many years after my interview with Bob Gutierrez, I would take ayahuasca, as described in subsequent chapters. It can be a terrifying and dangerous experience. Although I have gained insights through its use, I must add that people who practice psychonavigation have very similar experiences—without the physiological side effects and dangers.

An elder from the Salascan tribe, on the eastern slope of the Andes, once told me that psychotropic plants should be used like a corkscrew to

---

*Richard Evans Schultes and Robert F. Raffauf, *Vine of the Soul: Medicine Men, Their Plants and Rituals in the Columbian Amazonia* (Oracle, Ariz.: Synergetic Press, 1992), p. 4.

open a little hole in the tops of our heads. "After the hole is made," he said, "You don't need to take the potion anymore. All the knowledge just comes flowing in." I asked him if it were necessary to take psychotropic plants at all. He thought for a moment. "No," he said at last. "The knowledge is within all of us anyway. We must just open our heads to it and allow the dreams to pierce our thick skulls. There are many ways to do this." He went on to describe techniques and attitudes that are repeated throughout this book.

It is important to emphasize that ayahuasca as it is used by Amazonian cultures differs radically from hallucinogenic drugs taken for recreational purposes in "civilized" cultures. This difference is something that Schultes and many other authorities stress, and it is an area where they part company with the 1960s teachings of Timothy Leary. For the Amazonian, psychotropic plants are a vehicle for traveling into the sacred, for communicating with the natural and supernatural worlds and with the universal dream in which we are all united. Taking these plants provides not an escape from reality but rather a journey deep into the many realities that compose the oneness of all things, be they plant, animal, mineral, or spirit.

The idea that our positioning of humanity at the top of a pyramid is nothing more than a perception had never occured to me until that day with Bob Gutierrez. Much later I would learn that this view is very shamanic. If the world is as we dream it, then every reality is a matter of perception. We have dreamed it; therefore, it is. I have become convinced that everything we think and feel is merely a perception; that our lives—individually as well as communally—are molded around such perceptions; and that if we want to change, we must alter our perceptions. When we give our energy to a different dream, the world is transformed. To create a new world, we must first create a new dream.

Much of what I now know about the power of our dreams I have learned from another remarkable individual: an elder among the Shuar, an Amazonian tribe of headhunters.

2
The Shuar

I had first met members of the Shuar* tribe in 1968 when I was a Peace Corps volunteer helping Andean farmers colonize the Amazon basin. The Shuar were considered fierce warriors; I heard many stories about their raids, head-hunting, and savage rituals, although from personal encounters I found them to be a compassionate people who were gravely concerned about the impact colonists were having on the fragile rain forest ecology.

The town where I lived in 1968 was surrounded by jungle, a five-hour trek from the end of a mud road that wound its way down the eastern slopes of the Andes. Today the road runs through the center of the town; the jungle has disappeared.

Some Shuar have given up their traditional ways and have tried to adopt Western customs. For the most part, they live impoverished lives in oil company ghettos. Others, determined to maintain their independence, have moved deeper into the forest to places east of the Cutucú Mountains, an ancient mist-enshrouded range that long ago split away from the Andes and shifted its mammoth bulk toward the river-sea for which this vast region has been named.

In 1992 I decided to try to visit the Cutucú Shuar. I had just sold my alternative-energy company and was struggling with the guilt I had felt over all the years when, as a Peace Corps volunteer and as a consultant to the World Bank, I had promoted colonizing rain forests and constructing roads, dams, and other projects that had turned into ecological nightmares. I had grown painfully aware of the power in the message we had sent out to the world. "Become developed, like us," we had said. "Stop living in the Third World. Follow our example: join the First World." The only problem was that our example had destroyed many of the most beautiful places on our planet, and it threatened to upset completely the balance between humans

---

*Several books refer to the Shuar as the "Jivaro," a pejorative term meaning "rude" or "savage" and applied to the Shuar by their Spanish-speaking neighbors. Understandably, the Shuar themselves do not use the term.

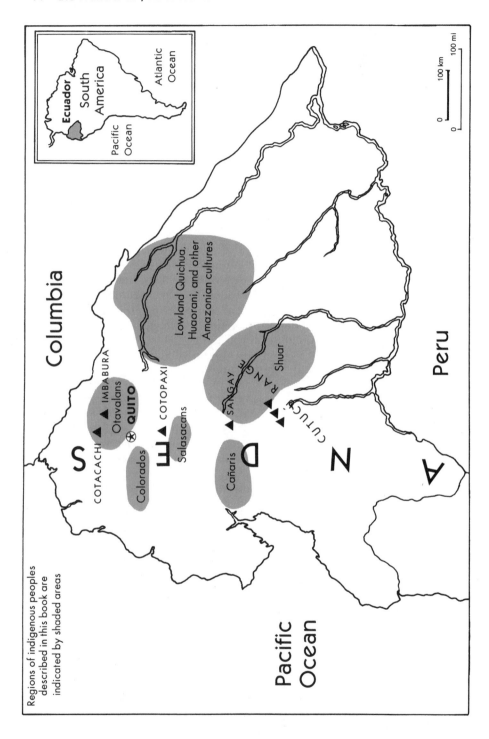

Regions of indigenous peoples described in this book are indicated by shaded areas

Columbia

Peru

Pacific Ocean

Ecuador
South America
Atlantic Ocean
Pacific Ocean

100 mi
100 km

COTACACHI
IMBABURA
Otavalans
QUITO
Colorados
COTOPAXI
Salasacans
Lowland Quichua, Huaorani, and other Amazonian cultures
SANGAY
Shuar
Cañaris
CUTUCU
ANDES

and nature. I hoped that I would learn something from the Cutucú Shuar. I was searching for a new direction in my own life and a way to right the wrongs that had been perpetrated by my generation.

That trip accomplished far more than I could ever have anticipated. It was the beginning of an extraordinary series of events. Over the next twenty months I would make repeated visits to the Shuar, the Lowland Quichua, and other Amazonian and Andean peoples. I would experience firsthand the way dreams and direct communication with nature, as well as inner voices, affect their daily lives.

I was told that my destination beyond the Cutucú was a five-day hike from the nearest road—five days for the Shuar, at least twice that for me. An Ecuadoran friend arranged for a single-engine missionary plane to take me in. Although I had done plenty of hiking in the rain forest during my Peace Corps days, this would be the first time I had ever flown low over the canopy deep into the jungle.

Not long after flying out of the little airstrip in the Upano Valley, I saw below the lines defining the frontier. To the west was the cleared land of the colonists, much of it still smoldering from slash-and-burn development. To the east lay solid, unbroken rain forest. The pilot turned to face me. "Those lines move farther out every day," he said, shaking his head sadly.

As soon as I could look below and see only vegetation, I felt a sense of relief. The rugged Cutucú reminded me of Tarzan's Lost World, another of my boyhood dreams materializing. The pilot shouted something I could not hear above the engine's roar and pointed at a tiny scar in the canopy. He headed directly for it, then banked, and I found myself looking down on a sight that took my breath away.

There below us in the middle of a clearing was a Shuar longhouse. Oval in shape, perhaps forty feet long, made of upright staves with a thatched roof, it might well have belonged to a North American Indian three hundred years ago. I recalled a late afternoon in a classroom with my seventh-grade teacher and scanned the clearing for a man with bow and arrow, but all I found was a stream running beside the house and what looked like small gardens scattered around it.

A sudden movement at the edge of the clearing caught my eye. My heart skipped a beat. My head bumped against the window as I tried to get a closer look. But no one appeared. Perhaps it had only been my imagination, or the shadow of a bird in flight. Still, I felt that Mrs. Simpson was close.

Then we were past the clearing. The pilot nosed the plane down toward the trees. He banked again. A path appeared in the jungle wall. With a start, I realized this was our landing strip. The plane dropped. Trees reached for

Photo by Ehud C. Sperling

FIGURE 1   Shuar longhouse, aerial view

our wingtips. We hit the ground, bounced, and raced through the jungle. Then we stopped. Through the window I saw what I had waited for.

A cluster of Shuar men stood at the edge of the dirt track. They wore T-shirts and cotton shorts, not the loincloths and headbands of former days. They watched us intently, their hair whipped by the wind from our propeller. I felt like an alien from another world.

As soon as the engine died, the pilot climbed out over the wing. I followed close behind. The Shuar stood quietly and waited. Their faces showed no sign of welcome or any other emotion. Once we reached them, I began introducing myself. Each shook my hand. Their attitude seemed to change. Several grinned broadly. One, a young man dressed more stylishly than the others in a print shirt, spoke in excellent Spanish. His name was Tomas, he said; he attended the university in Quito and was home on vacation. I was very welcome. He ushered me away from the plane, to the edge of the landing strip.

"You wait here," he said, a gold tooth flashing in the sun. "When the plane is unpacked, we will go downriver in canoes." He pointed to a narrow hole in the foliage at the edge of the jungle.

I nodded my agreement. He returned to the plane, where his companions had already begun unloading burlap bags and wooden crates. I watched for several minutes, then ambled over to a hole in the jungle wall. An enticing path, resembling a tunnel, led into the forest. I tried to peer in, but found only darkness.

I wasn't helping by simply waiting, so I stepped inside. It was cool and

Photo by John Perkins

FIGURE 2   Shuar longhouse, ground view

quiet. The smell of plants and damp soil enveloped me. An occasional bird call was all that broke the silence in surroundings that felt distinctly mythical. I wandered on. A butterfly fluttered up and alighted on my shoulder. The path took an abrupt turn, and before me was a long, white sandy beach sloping to a swiftly flowing river.

Two dugout canoes were pulled onto the beach. Drawn to them, I felt the urge to touch them both. I went and stood between them and allowed my hands to explore their rough gunwales. They were well used, full of nicks and bruises, yet about them was the feeling that they were valued, even loved. They were carefully patched in places. Paddles lying in them were beautifully crafted, their blades shaped like giant hearts, or perhaps palm leaves.

Suddenly I felt a man's presence behind me. I turned to see him standing with his back to the jungle.

He had a shock of white hair. He wore no shirt, and his wrinkled skin led me to guess his age at over eighty. But it was his eyes that most amazed me. Deeply set and brilliant, they conveyed a sense of wisdom and of sadness. I thought I sensed in them a timeless knowledge that was at once hypnotic and frightening. "I am Numi," he said as he extended a weathered hand. "In Spanish, my first name is Alberto. You must be the gringo we're expecting."

I had heard much about him during the days I had spent preparing for this trip. Himself part Shuar, he was married to a full-blood Shuar.

Photo by Ehud C. Sperling

FIGURE 3   River scene with Shuar dugouts

Although a former teacher at the Catholic mission school, he was considered a powerful shaman. Above all, people spoke of him as a compassionate human being, a true teacher who formed a bridge between cultures.

He sat down on the edge of a dugout and motioned for me to do the same. Then he began asking questions. He was easy to be open with. His questions didn't pry; they were asked in the manner of a person deeply interested in learning. He was, I sensed, accustomed to helping others with their problems.

He confided that he had tried to return to civilization several times. "It's just too rough," he said. "I'm not tough enough for that kind of life."

I laughed at that. "Where I come from," I told him, "we think of the jungle as rough. If you can live here, you can survive anywhere."

He shook his head and turned to look down the river.

"I know what you mean, though," I continued. "I've grown discouraged by the materialism of my culture. The crime, the divorce, the greed and pollution."

"You have lost touch with Mother," he said. He stood up, held out his arms, and turned in a slow circle.

I watched him in silence. He clenced his hands into fists and drew them to his heart. "Now it begins to hurt."

"Yes." Incidents from my own life came to mind. "I sometimes think that all we care about is money and dominating things. Other people. Other countries. Nature. That we've lost the ability to love."

His eyes met mine, a stern look. "You haven't lost the ability." They held mine for the longest moment. Finally they turned away, to the jungle on the far bank.

"The world is as you dream it," he said at last. He walked to the edge of the water. "Your people dreamed of huge factories, tall buildings, as many cars as there are raindrops in this river. Now you begin to see that your dream is a nightmare." He bent to pick up a stone. "The problem is your country is like this pebble." He threw it far out into the river. "Everything you do ripples across the Mother."

I went to stand next to him. "I've seen the line where the destruction ends and the jungle begins." I thought about my own selfish life, the negative dreams I had given my energy to. "It's a terrible thing. We have forced our greed into your world."

This brought an unexpected chuckle. "Yes," he said. He peered deep into my eyes. "But you want it to be different. Now you must learn to change. Perhaps that's why you've come, to learn from us."

"How can I change, Don Alberto? How can my people change this terrible situation we've created?"

His eyes held mine once again. "That's simple," he replied. "All you have to do is change the dream."

It sounded so easy. "How long will that take?"

He glanced once more down the river. "It can be accomplished in a generation. You need only plant a different seed, teach your children to dream new dreams." He placed a hand on my shoulder. "I will introduce you to people who can help."

Outside, the jungle was waking. A cacophony of bird calls was my alarm clock. I opened my eyes to the soft light that penetrated the palm walls of the shaman Kenkuim's lodge. A rooster crowed somewhere off in the distance. As I stretched, I disturbed the banana leaves that covered the dirt floor beneath my sleeping bag, causing them to crackle like tiny fires. I remembered waking up once during the night. All had been dark except for a flickering light that I had believed was from a candle, until I had noticed a shadow seated in the corner and heard the music of a bamboo flute. I had called out to Kenkuim, but when no one answered, I wondered if it might be one of the spirits the Shuar claim roam the forests at night, often visiting the homes of powerful shamans. At first I had been frightened but then, feeling no sense of malice, had fallen asleep to the melody of the flute.

Now, in the morning's gentle light, the lodge seemed transformed. There was no sign of my apparition; neither his flute nor his candle was anywhere to be seen. I suspected it had been a mere mortal after all. Although Kenkuim's family was very quiet, I knew by the familiar sounds that they were preparing breakfast behind the wooden screen that separated the cooking area from the ceremonial circle, the place where I had been privileged to sleep. I heard the telltale giggles of a child and the rattle of a pot as it was lifted from the fire. The smell of wood smoke reminded me of autumn mornings in New Hampshire and my boyhood dream of living with Indians.

I realized that it was mid-October 1992 and recalled a day in 1952 when I had played an Indian chief welcoming Columbus to my second-grade class. Five hundred years, almost to the day, since that fateful landing—and here I was with an Indian family in the Amazon! It seemed unbelievable. Wanting the moment to last, I rolled over and pulled the edge of my sleeping bag up to cover my head. I listened to the sounds of the jungle and the Shuar family. I drank in the variety of aromas and thought about that Italian adventurer who had claimed these lands for Spain. A hero in 1492 and also 1952, Columbus was a different person in 1992.

I heard footsteps and, peering out from beneath a corner of my sleeping bag, saw a little face. It screamed in glee and scampered away. I knew I should rouse myself, but decided to take a few more minutes to just lie there and listen to the sounds, smell the odors, and think about this day.

Columbus's image in 1992 was tarnished. Some blamed him for the genocide of America's indigenous people and the destruction of her forests. While Columbus had certainly exploited the people of the Caribbean for his own gain, he had died nearly five hundred years ago, long before

Photo by Ehud C. Sperling

FIGURE 4   Shuar child

the destruction that had happened during my lifetime because industries needed oil, wood, cattle, gold, and other resources to feed the appetites of seemingly insatiable modern cultures.

I turned onto my back and looked up at the high thatched roof, blackened by the fires that were kept constantly burning, not only for cooking but also because the smoke helps maintain contact with ancestors who have become the rain or birds, plants, and animals.

The Shuar believe that their ancestors are always available to act as guides and teachers. They seek answers to practical questions as well as general advice about how to live their lives. The thought occurred to me that the spirit of Columbus could teach us today a lesson or two about this world he had done so much to define.

In the late 1400s many people believed the world was round, although they acted as though it were flat. Commerce, politics, philosophy, religion, and war were based on flat-world concepts. The fear of going too far and falling off imposed physical restrictions. The same fear also acknowledged human frailty while glorifying the mystery of the unknown. Mariners' charts depicting gigantic dragons around the borders humbled men before the powers of nature.

As soon as Columbus returned to Spain, all that changed. If the abyss did not exist, if you would not fall off into the jaws of monsters, and if instead you could simply keep going until you returned home, then where was the mystery? Columbus's voyages in effect removed the barrier of fear that held back his contemporaries from testing their physical and perceptual limitations. Global exploration was an outward manifestation of new perceptions concerning science and the human role in the world.

Lying there contemplating the smoke as it rose to the blackened ceiling, I reflected on the message brought by Columbus's spirit. The issue in my mind was not whether Columbus was a hero or a villain, but that he had the courage to go out and prove what many knew to be the truth. Like the people of his time, many of us today allow a false perception to control our lives. The mentality of mining and polluting the Earth, constantly building higher mountains of material wealth to satisfy our greed, and believing that science can heal all wounds, is our equivalent of a flat-world outlook. Yet many of us are unsure of how to implement a new way of relating to the Earth. We need someone to act as a new Columbus today, to open up our perceptions of a new global ecology.

A shadow passed across my vision. The little face peered down at me again. I sat up and the child handed me a banana, then pivoted and ran back behind the wooden screen.

Numi's words returned to me: "The world is as you dream it." As long as the dream had been of a flat world, this land simply had not existed for Europe. As long as we dream of short-term economic growth at the expense of long-term sustainability and spirituality, the destruction of this beautiful planet—our home—will go on.

I finished off the banana. What will it take, I wondered, to replace the old, ultimately self-destructive dream with one that recognizes our essential unity with all other things?

I stood and stretched. I rolled up my sleeping bag and walked over to the palm-pole wall. Like all Shuar houses, this one had been designed so that you could easily see out through the spaces between the staves. The jungle was right there. The bird calls were loud. I had that same feeling I had had as a boy, one that was difficult to pin down but was tied to the kinship I felt with the forests and people who live in them as guests rather than adversaries.

I turned and walked around the wooden screen. The Shuar family was congregated about the breakfast fire. Kenkuim, the shaman, sat on his wooden stool. It had been carved from a single tree stump in the shape of a turtle to represent the live turtle that served as a seat for Tsúnkqui, the mythological first shaman and goddess of the water. Kenkuim glanced in my direction. He stood up and waved for me to join them.

Marta, the oldest child, jumped up and ran to me. She took my hand and led me toward the fire. I felt privileged to be in the presence of these people. I felt like I belonged with them in their forest home.

Whenever I am in a forest, I become intensely aware of my physical limitations. Without a car, refrigerator, or stove, I am a different person from the one I was raised to be. Covering a mere five miles can tax my every muscle. Preparing a meal becomes an almost impossible burden, until I accept it as a sacred ceremony, a type of meditation. The butterfly travels faster than I do; the worm is a more efficient forager.

After completing a day of trekking and the evening meal, I feel a great sense of accomplishment, a kind of euphoria. It is easy to lie back and, looking into the high canopy, speculate on the incredible intelligence of the forest itself or the power that brought it—us—into being. What engineer could have designed such a sophisticated system? What architect could have envisioned such variety and beauty?

One evening, as the sun dropped below a jungle-enshrouded mountain, I found myself watching my two Shuar companions clean up after our meal and wondering how my ancestors emerged from a forest somewhere in the world that had probably been similar to this one. I lay on top of my sleeping bag, exhausted from a six-hour hike along muddy trails and up a glacier-fed river. My clothes were strung out to dry in a small lean-to behind me.

In the emerging darkness beyond our camp, fireflies warmed up their batteries. The little lanterns flickering silent messages among the trees took my mind off my burning feet and battered muscles. I felt my body relax, felt a sense of well-being spreading through me. Then a cramp gripped my calf. As I massaged it, I watched my two friends tirelessly working. Their faces radiant in the firelight, they talked and laughed in voices so subdued that the jungle barely noticed. How different we were, not only in the ways we related to the world around us but also in our bodies. Much taller and, by appearances, stronger than they, I had been fed the industrial world's most nutritious foods, educated at the best of schools. Yet here I lay, incapacitated by a walk that was as routine for them as driving to the office was for me. The apparent irony struck me as humorous. Then another thought came: that they and I were really just alike, composed of identical atoms and chemicals.

"We see the world with different eyes," I said to myself, then realized that it was not our eyes at all that were different; it was the way we looked through them.

One of them came to me, his hands cupped in front of him. He lowered them to my sleeping bag. "It flew too close to the fire," he said. There at the corner of my sleeping bag was a firefly, its light extinguished. "Let it rest."

I watched as it began to move slowly about, like a dazed boxer trying to pull himself from the mat. Then, miraculously, its light began to glow—weakly at first, then stronger, until after several minutes it had restored itself to normal. It seemed to acknowledge me in some way before it flew away. I watched it until it disappeared into the blackness that now blanketed the forest. I wondered what made it glow and realized that it too was composed of the same chemicals as I.

I glanced around at the diversity of this place where I would spend the night. Beneath the plumage, the foliage, and the decorations was a common base. Somewhere, far back in time, we all had emerged from the same seed. Feeling close to the trees and ferns, the soil and rocks, the birds and insects, and to the earth herself, I lay back and closed my eyes. The voices of the two Shuar men lulled me. I felt drowsy and peaceful.

I must have drifted off for a moment. Then I sat up with a start and swatted at something on my foot. Glancing down, I discovered a parade of ants. I jumped up, brushed myself off from head to toe, and shook out my sleeping bag. My companions smiled at me and continued their conversation. Before spreading my sleeping bag out again, I swept the ants and leaves away with my hands, exposing the bare dirt beneath. Satisfied that I had cleaned the area as thoroughly as possible, I lay down again. I assured myself that they were gone and, closing my eyes, concentrated on the sounds.

The ants did not take long to return. I felt them exploring my feet. Although they did not bite me, their tickling drove me crazy. I began to fret. How could I sleep with them tormenting me? What if they started biting? Were they poisonous? Finally, when I realized there was little I could do about them, I decided to resign myself to their presence. I figured they were with me for the night and I would have to accommodate them. I focused my full attention on them. If I could not get rid of them, I told myself, I would join them.

I remembered a story I had heard about an Apache warrior who was captured by Comanches. He was stripped and his limbs were stretched out and tied to stakes in the ground. His entire body was painted with honey. The Comanches then left him to the mercy of the ants.

At first their bites infuriated him. He struggled desperately to free himself. But once he understood that there was no way for him to break loose, he decided to look at the world from the ants' perspective. He projected himself into them. As they ate away at him, he visualized himself turning into an ant. Things he had taken for granted—pebbles, dewdrops, his own skin—took on new meaning. Suddenly he was overwhelmed with a feeling of ecstasy, for he felt himself becoming reunited, through the ants, with his mother, the Earth. He was not merely becoming an ant, he was connecting directly with all of nature. He had visions of ancestors who came down and began to chant by his side.

The Apache warrior began to sing. His powerful voice carried on the wind all the way to where the Comanches had made their evening camp. Furtive looks shot around the fire. The Apache chant made the Comanches nervous, for it was common knowledge that the gods did not smile on warriors who killed a crazy person.

The Comanches hurried back to their prisoner. Covered with ants and blood, he was nevertheless calm, his expression that of a man at peace. He continued to sing in a loud, joyous voice. Immediately they cut his bonds and carried him to the river.

He did not seem at all thankful when they washed the honey, ants, and blood away. He sat down on the bank and stared into the river. So the Comanches left him.

Eventually, the Apache returned to his people. He taught them about the beauty of the smallest of things: ants, grains of sand, the veins on a leaf. He taught them to love such things and to call upon them for guidance. People from far away came to seek the advice of this powerful shaman.

I opened my eyes. One of my Shuar friends was looking down at me. "You like to sleep with ants?" he asked.

I shrugged. "They came by themselves."

He stepped over to the packs we had carried in and bent down. When he stood, he was holding a stubby stick. With his machete he whittled away the skin and I recognized it as sugar cane. He carried it several yards into

Photo by Ehud C. Sperling

FIGURE 5   Sacred waterfall of the Shuar

the jungle and set it on an old tree stump. "No more ants in your sleeping bag," he said. "They will be happy now."

The sacred waterfall of the Shuar is breathtaking and beautiful. Yet standing before it, looking up into the rainbow that arches through the cascading waters, the visitor is struck by a feeling that transcends the magnificence of the landscape. No matter what your religion, you cannot help but sense the spirit of this place. Its power defies any attempt to describe the euphoria inspired by a natural phenomenon so overwhelmingly grand that its voice seems to cross all the bridges of time, speaking to us from some ancient past as well as from the unknown future.

Getting to the sacred waterfall had taken Tantar and me the better part of a day. It had been an exhausting hike, mostly uphill, through dense jungle, mud, and rushing rivers and along the sides of treacherous ledges. The last hour had been the most difficult as we had picked our way down the slippery rock face into a canyon that had been chiseled out of the rose-colored granite by the ceaseless energy of the river herself.

Now we stood there, looking up into the mists through the rainbow known as Tuntiak and up to where the icy waters broke out of the forests at the lip of the great cliff some three hundred feet above. The sky was beginning to show the magenta streaks of evening, and the rainbow appeared to turn darker before our very eyes. This was indeed a sacred place, for it was from Tuntiak that the first Shuar man and woman had emerged. They had been created simultaneously and equal, not—as I had been told by people who had heard the Christian Creation story—one after the other.

We removed our clothes and slipped into the deep pool at the foot of the waterfall. The roar was deafening. The frigid river at first stunned, then revived, us. I caught myself on the verge of screaming my exhilaration but was stopped by the recollection of Tantar's admonition that we must show quiet respect at all times. We splashed each other in a sort of ritual and swam to the waterfall; as we clung to rock outcroppings we lay our heads back, mouths open to drink the spray, careful to avoid the full force of the falling water.

Refreshed, we stood in the waning afternoon sunlight. The warmth penetrated, as though we and the waterfall and all the jungle around shared the embers of an eternal flame whose energy originated in each of us and at the same time was part of a greater unity. Although invisible, it was an ever-present bond every bit as real as the mist rising from the pool up through the rainbow and into the sunset-tinted clouds.

Tantar pointed into the pool. "Tsúnkqui is there," he said. He told the story of the water goddess who rides on the back of a giant turtle and is guarded by a wall of crocodiles and anacondas. "I have never taken a fish we did not need for our hunger; she will protect us," he said matter-of-factly, then showed me a wonderful smile.

Until this trip, I had known Tantar only by his Christian name, Pedro. He was twenty-three years old, spoke fluent Spanish, had completed high school at the Catholic mission, and was—as far as I had been able to discern—fully committed to the "new Shuar way" promoted by the mission priests. During the past eight hours I had begun to see a different side of Tantar.

We walked slowly away from the waterfall, along a narrow and slippery trail that led to the lean-to where we would spend the night.

"Tell me more about the Shuar gods," I urged.

He gave me a fleeting glance. For a long moment, he remained silent, then he sighed. "They are beautiful," he said at last. "Especially the women."

We walked on. I prompted him to explain. "I have often wondered," he said, "why Catholics don't worship any women gods. For us they are so beautiful, and they are necessary to keep the men in line." He pointed

FIGURE 6 Shuar gods and goddesses

out that Shuar men have always been famous for their fighting abilities. "We are fierce. But our ferocity must be channeled." He explained that Núnkui was the goddess of plants, gardens, and food, and that she also inspired Shuar women to control their men, preventing needless feuds, overhunting, and the clearing of forests. "No plant or tree should be cut unless it is essential to do so, and never without Núnkui's permission."

I asked him if Shuar men and women were considered equal.

He gave me a quizzical look. Then he started to giggle. Cupping his hands over his breasts, he shook with laughter. "Equal!" he exclaimed at last. "No." He then grew more serious. "Can I have a baby?" he asked. "Can you?" He paused as we emerged onto a rocky cliff with a spectacular view of the sacred waterfall bathed in the orange-and-red glow of the setting equatorial sun. "Men are strong like the waterfall," he said, pointing. "Women nourish the earth. They create life. They are the sunset that hugs the waterfall and soothes it to sleep."

"But which is more important?"

His face showed surprise. "You can't have one without the other."

I began to understand that my questions did not have the same meaning for him as for me. So I changed my approach and asked whether there was ever tension between the sexes, any ambiguity in roles. He explained that the god Jémpe took care of such issues. "Whenever men and women are together, Jémpe is there to maintain balance." His eyes wandered to the waterfall. "Balance is the most important thing—between men and women, adults and children, people and plants and animals." His eyes met mine. "Balance."

We stood together watching the play of the changing colors on the waterfall. The forest seemed to be waking up as the day retired. From all around came the sounds of renewed life: the shrieks of birds, buzz of insects, and in the distance the howl of a monkey.

"Etsáa," Tantar said, indicating the place where the sun had sunk behind the cliffs, "leaves us now."

He walked to the edge of the rock and stared off into the distance. Again I was filled with a sensation of warmth, almost as though Tsúnkqui, Núnkui, Jémpe, and Etsáa were surrounding me and radiating a physical energy that penetrated deep within me. I started toward him.

Suddenly my knees buckled. Perhaps it was simple exhaustion. Shivering, I tried to focus on the darkening sky, tried to think about the sunset over my home in the United States, tried to get in touch with a reality that seemed very distant.

Sensing my quandary, Tantar hurried back to my side. "Our gods are beautiful," he said, and the sound of his voice was reassuring. He touched my arm and together we sat down on the rock. My vertigo passed.

"You will like the story of Etsáa." he said. He explained that Etsáa had once spent all his time with the Shuar. He had protected them from the Evias, a tribe of ferocious giant cannibals, by hunting with his blowgun and providing food for the Evias so they would not eat the Shuar. Then, through trickery, Etsáa had killed the Evias. He had blown life through his blowgun back into all the animals he had fed to the Evias. Tantar smiled. "Once again, balance was restored." After that, Etsáa had risen on a lightning bolt into the heavens; from there he watched over the Shuar during the day.

"And at night?" I asked.

"Etsáa sent the god Ayumpum, who taught us to boil the vine ayahuasca so we can communicate directly with the plants and animals. Ayahuasca is a gift from Etsáa. It opens our hearts, frees our souls, helps us feel our oneness with the rocks, the animals, the plants, and each other. So we are never alone, not even at night." He stood and spread his arms. "We are all here."

The night was dry, with no sign of rain. We lay in the open, several yards away from the lean-to, vying with each other to see who could count the most shooting stars. We could hear the waterfall. I was about to ask Tantar whether Tuntiak was still there when I realized that my question was as foolish as the one about the equality of the sexes. Of course Tuntiak was always there, whether visible to humans or not.

"Your gods are beautiful," I said aloud. I felt his eyes move down from the sky toward mine. "You know," I continued, "I believe Catholics have women gods too. They just don't realize it."

"How sad for them," he said.

"I agree."

I heard him sigh. "I like to fall asleep with women gods," he said. "They help me dream wonderful dreams." There was a long pause. "Dreams come true."

Looking back up into a sky that was alive with stars, I thought about Tsúnkqui and Núnkui. If everyone fell asleep thinking about them, the world would be a very different place. Then an image formed before me. I saw a television set. A parade of advertisements flashed across it: automobiles, hair spray, oven cleaners, decongestants, soft drinks, things obtained from mining the Earth, things the people of my culture see before falling asleep. I wondered why we had turned our dreams over to a handful of greedy business executives.

I promised myself that I would talk with Numi about this. Perhaps he could help my people regain control over our dreams.

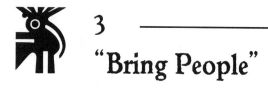

3
"Bring People"

Numi and I each had a hammock. We swung slowly back and forth next to the fire. It was early afternoon and the tropical jungle heat was suffocating, but a Shuar lodge is never without its fire. The spirits were present.

Our hammocks were tied at one end to the central pole and at the other to separate support poles in the outer wall, like spokes radiating out from the hub of a wheel. To the Shuar the central pole is far more than a structural support that holds up the roof, for it represents the Cosmic Tree, the Tree of Life, connecting the upper world with the middle and lower worlds. It is a sacred place that provides both an entryway for spirits to visit this world and a ladder for us to travel to parallel worlds. The fire near the central pole is an additional inducement to the spirits, who, according to Shuar beliefs, are attracted by fire and smoke. The fire also serves as a beacon to help psychonavigational travelers find their way home. At certain times, such as during festivals and funerals for powerful men, the central pole plays a strong role in rituals. People who sleep in hammocks that are tied to the Cosmic Tree are likely to receive dream messages that are sent to them directly by the entities residing in the upper and lower worlds.

Our heads were near the central pole, close together, so we could talk without raising our voices. The fire, crackling in the afternoon heat, was built as Shuar fires are always built, at the junction of three thick trunks that form a Y. A spider monkey frolicked in the high rafters of the thatched roof above us.

It was the last day of this particular visit, and already, like reverse déjà vu, I had a strong sense of the nostalgia that would overwhelm me when I arrived at Miami International Airport and began my journey back into the heart of my technological culture. I knew the guilt I would suffer over the miles of asphalt and concrete, the self-disgust inspired by the massive overpasses that had wiped out acres upon acres of Everglades and that had been erected as much for my benefit as anyone else's and had been built with my tax payments. Preparing for it was impossible, but discussing it with Numi helped dissipate some of the anxiety.

We talked about the good fortune I had enjoyed in life, of dreams that had been realized. I told Numi about "Trail to the North," Mrs. Simpson, and the photo of the man with the bow and arrow. I reminisced about my days as an international consultant. He asked questions about Iran and Indonesia. He seemed more interested in desert Bedouins than in the jungle denizens of Borneo and Papua New Guinea. I described the terror I had felt when it appeared that the alternative-energy company I had founded would go bankrupt, and the happiness when instead we completed our first multimillion dollar project. I emphasized the role that the project had played in cleaning up acid rain. "Now," I said, "I have sold it."

He reached across the space between the hammocks to shake my hand. "You are free of all that," he laughed, sharing my obvious enthusiasm.

"Yes," I agreed. "And here I am. I have come home. What can I do to help save this beautiful forest?"

He hesitated. His hand grasped the edge of my hammock; the swing of his slowed. "What do you want to do?" He stopped swinging altogether.

Taking a cue from earlier conversations, I mentioned the Shuar's dependence on what they call the evil cow. "Your people hate clearing jungle to create pasture for beef cattle. Maybe I can help find an alternative. Iguana farms have been successful in Panama and Colombia. Iguanas live in the forest, off native plants." He was silent. "Or perhaps I could explore the possibility of drying fruits for export. Or herbal medicines."

He resumed his swinging. "What got us started raising cattle?" he asked.

"The missionaries."

"Yes, and the government colonization laws that give land title to people who cut trees and create farms. Do you know where those laws came from?"

I did. They were modeled after the U.S. Homestead Act of the late 1800s. I felt the guilt slide in and settle as a lump near my heart.

"That's right," he said. "And more colonists come because of the roads that are built by your oil, lumber, and mining companies." He lay back and looked up at the roof. My eyes followed his to where the monkey sat on a rafter, chewing on what looked like a piece of sugar cane. "If you want to help us," he said slowly and deliberately, "if you want to help these forests, then you should start with your own people. It is your people more than mine who need to change."

I knew he was right and knew also that I had understood for some time what he just now had verbalized. "I see what you mean," I said, then asked whether he could help me.

His answer came as a shock. It took me back to a discussion with three French tour guides in a restaurant in Quito the night before I had flown into the Amazon. I had argued vehemently against bringing foreigners into the jungle, in favor of allowing the Shuar to stay isolated. They had maintained that the rain forest is a classroom to be shared.

"Bring people," he said. "Bring your people to us. We can help change that dream you have of huge factories, tall buildings, and more automobiles than there are grains of sand."

I was incredulous. "You want tourists to come in here?"

"No." He smiled gently. "Not tourists, John. Bring in people who want to learn." He emphasized the last four words, then repeated them, adding that the Shuar have much to teach about the way the world is dreamed and that the people of the United States and other northern countries have a great deal to learn. He went on to explain that outsiders have tried to change the Shuar for centuries. "They told us our language was bad, we must learn Spanish, and now English and German. Our religion was wrong, we must convert to Christianity." As he said this he crossed himself. "Our way of life was primitive, we must cut the forests and raise cattle. The message our young people hear from the foreigner is that the Shuar ways are no good." Eloquently he made the case that people coming to learn would also help the Shuar maintain their dream. "Our young people will understand," he said, "that the Shuar way is a true way."

He turned in his hammock and looked me straight in the eye. "You and I," he said, "know that Mother Earth will survive. But if the people who call themselves 'civilized' continue to dream their greedy dreams, Mother Earth will shake us all off like fleas. Many other animals and plants will go with us. Many have already gone. We must try to change that. The dream of your people must change." He pushed back into his hammock and began to swing.

We lay there in silence, each of us lost in his own thoughts. The fire crackled. I closed my eyes for a moment. When I opened them, the monkey had disappeared. I searched the rafters, but could find no sign of him.

"What kind of people, Don Alberto?"

He took his time at answering me. "That is for you to decide," he said at last. "They are your people. You have been educated in the same ways as them." He fell silent, and I thought about the hours I had spent in sunless classrooms, about the endless theoretical discussions, and about the society this approach to education had produced. Visions of fouled air, polluted rivers, and forests devastated in the name of progress danced before my eyes.

"We are only five percent of the world's population. We use over thirty percent of many of Mother Earth's most precious resources," I said.

His hammock started moving again, but he made no comment. I thought about a Shuar boy who, after cutting himself on a machete two days earlier, had gone into the jungle with his father to gather leaves for a poultice. This very morning I had examined the wound; it had healed nicely, without any infection. That boy would think twice before destroying a plant. How different from the way I had been treated when, at about the same age, I had cut myself with a jackknife! To this day I do not know where most of the medicines I use come from.

"I'll bring people," I said.

"Good." He rose slowly from his hammock and patted my knee. "But only those who want to learn." He walked over to the fire and peered into its embers. "Come now," he said. "Let's catch a fish for dinner."

Part ❋ Two

Manco

Manco sat very still. An old man, he felt secure like a baby bathed in the warmth of Inti, the setting sun. He watched Inti's golden cape spread swiftly across the sacred mountain to the West. Soon it would be dark. His work would begin.

He had chosen this spot carefully, for Sinchi had told him he would need all the power Pachamama, Mother Earth, could give him. The memory of Sinchi brought a smile to his wrinkled face. Now he, Manco, was an elder. It seemed only yesterday that he had made his run and entered the proud ranks of the quipo camayocs. Before long, he knew, he would follow once again in the footsteps of Sinchi. But for now, it was enough that he seek his teacher's advice and perhaps a gift of power.

He listened to the wind in the trees and absorbed the energy that was generated by the two mountains, Grandfather Imbabura in front and Grandmother Cotocachi behind him. He felt the love that surrounded him as it flowed through his body. The energy of the mountains was balanced, male and female. He would need them both. He closed his eyes. He would fly as the eagle, the way Sinchi had taught him.

Slowly, the energy began to lift him. The wind sang as it passed through the feathers of his wings. Higher and higher he rose. He felt exhilarated. Offering thanks to both Inti and his teacher, he looked down on the land he loved so much.

His village was small. It became a speck and then disappeared into the mountains, the sacred mountains, the ones that were part of him, part of the dream of his ancestors. He glided high above them, into Inti.

Sinchi emerged from the sun. Although his appearance was not unexpected, his presence was always marvelous, an event of great power that took Manco by surprise. Sinchi carried his golden staff and waved it before him. His energy, like that of Inti, radiated through Manco.

Suddenly Sinchi was right next to him. Manco could smell his familiar smell and feel his breath. In his hand Sinchi held a tiny leather pouch. "A new birth," Sinchi said, thrusting the pouch into Manco's hand. "You are mother and father."

Manco bowed and took the pouch. He thanked his teacher. Then, again, he became the eagle.

He returned to the place between Grandmother Cotocachi and Grandfather Imbabura. He sat watching the last rays of Inti fade into the purple haze of the coming night.

Before long, he heard a sound that reminded him of a growling jaguar. Deep and guttural, it took him back to the time when as a young man he had accompanied Sinchi on the long and difficult journey into the Amazon jungle to spend a month working with Shuar shamans. One night while in an ayahuasca trance, he had come face to face with an immense female jaguar. The animal had jumped down from a tree into the path, where she blocked his passage. They had stood there staring into each other's eyes.

The animal's growl had been like no other sound he had ever heard either before or after. It had chilled him to the bone and silenced all the birds, animals, and even insects, as though every living creature had stopped in its tracks or sneaked off to hide in a dark cave, under a log, or in whatever shelter it could find. The growl had terrified him and also held him spellbound, a prisoner to it and to the incredible animal before him.

They had confronted each other for what seemed an eternity. Then the jaguar had pawed the air with her huge front paws and leaped back into the tree. Manco had quickly returned to the shaman's lodge and been told that the jaguar's visit was a sign; he was now ready to become a powerful healer, not only of bodies but also of souls—and more important, he was to be a restorer of balance between the worlds of spirit, nature, and people.

Now he heard the growl again. He closed his eyes and in his mind watched the place where Inti had set below the mountains, watched as the big bus—grander than any he had ever seen—pulled up in front of his home. It towered above the adobe walls and the thatching he and his family had woven into the roof. A thing from another world, it growled like the jungle cat, and he knew that the people in it who had journeyed from this other world had come to learn from him as he himself had learned from the jaguar. The door opened; like a Spanish shield it caught a final ray from Inti's crown and flashed a path of bright light down the mountain slope to the spot where he sat.

A woman stepped out of the bus. Then a man. They were followed by what seemed like a parade of giant people, carrying leather cases and cameras. Manco had seen gringos before, but never so many all together. He studied them with the care of an experienced quipu camayoc, sending his spirit into each to help him better understand how he could assist their healing. He felt their energy and understood why they had come.

Manco opened his eyes and slowly stood. Above him the stars shone with fierce intensity. He bowed in the direction of sleeping Inti and, turning, headed up the hill toward his home. He had much to do before their arrival materialized. But as he ascended the winding path, his mind did not dwell on them; he thought instead about his own teacher, the tiny leather pouch, and the words. He would be both mother and father to the new birth.

4
Preparation

The vision quest is a spiritual journey to wisdom that has been practiced by people for as long as history can remember. The resulting visions are recorded in cave drawings and described in the oral traditions of cultures throughout the world. Native North Americans believed that animals took vision quests when they hibernated during the long winter months. Christ's forty days in the wilderness was a vision quest. Many of the prayers, meditations, and rituals used by the world's religions originally were developed as vehicles for the vision quest.

Before my discussions with Numi I had devoted a great deal of time to studying shamanic journeys, vision quests, the many variations of them, and their modern applications. I understood that what Numi had in mind was a vision quest for contemporary North Americans. We and the other "moderns" on this planet are perhaps the first people in history not to practice some form of the vision quest as a regular part of our educational process. Numi wanted to see this turned around.

Yet his request created in me a personal conflict. Taking North Americans into the rain forest was counter to my belief that the Shuar, Huaorani, Lowland Quichua, and other peoples should be left alone.

I struggled with this dilemma for several months. I sought the advice of friends who shared many of my concerns, but who also helped me understand that the rain forest people could no longer remain isolated and that, unless we northerners change our vision, the rain forests are doomed. If the jungles vanish, my friends pointed out, the cultures of the Shuar and their neighbors will have no hope of surviving. With the forests intact, those people will at least have options. I became convinced that changing the consciousness of my own people was essential for the preservation of rain forests and that the vision quest might play an important role in this process. In any case, I was committed to honoring the promise I had made to Numi.

I also dreamed recurrently about an old Otavalan shaman named Manco who lived high in the Andes. He was on a vision quest, and in my dream he transformed himself into an eagle. He appeared to beckon, as if he wanted me to come to him. I remembered being haunted, while I was a Middlebury student, by a dream of an Indian boy running through mountains. The two, I knew, were connected.

Finally, after much soul-searching, I decided to take a group to visit Numi. But this decision created another quandary. How was I to honor his requirement that I take in only people who want to learn? Who was to make the determination? Fortunately I was to find help from two sources: an old college friend and an organization also dedicated to sharing the wisdom of indigenous peoples with the "developed" countries of the North.

Gary Margolis was much more than an associate professor of English. He was also a brilliant poet with a deep philosophical as well as artistic interest in the effect language has on peoples' attitudes toward culture and the environment. Perhaps most important, he was a psychologist who headed up Middlebury College's counseling services. And he was a former classmate of mine.

Gary and I had not seen or heard from each other for twenty-five years. Then, one day not long after *The Stress-Free Habit* was published, Gary called me. "Imagine, a Middlebury dropout writing such a wonderful book!" he chided. We talked at length, and he asked many questions about the cultures from which I had learned techniques for managing stress. In particular, he inquired about the difficulties involved in getting to Ecuador.

"It takes three and a half hours by plane from Miami."

"So close," he mused, "yet so far away. Truly a different world, a separate reality."

That summer, during a trip to visit my parents in New Hampshire, I drove to Middlebury. Gary and I spent several hours together. I gave him a copy of *Psychonavigation,* which had just been published.

Several weeks later he phoned. "Is it really that beautiful?" he asked, referring to Ecuador.

"Words can't describe it," I told him.

" feel I must go there," he said.

Much later in the year he called again to tell me he was considering applying for a grant to study the influence language has on behavior. "I would like to go to Ecuador to visit some of your friends, John—the Quechua and Shuar." Half in jest, not really believing it would ever happen, I promised to escort him personally.

Gary did receive his grant. At first I was somewhat dismayed by the prospects of taking him to Ecuador. But then his enthusiasm calmed me, for he had called on a morning when I had woken up particularly concerned about my obligation to take to the Shuar only people who wanted to learn. As we talked, Gary's excitement empowered me. It helped me appreciate the privileged position I was in and to recognize it for what it truly was: an honor rather than an obligation, an opportunity and challenge to be met, not a burden to be avoided.

I discussed my situation with him, realizing even as I did so that I was dealing with a rare personality. Gary was a friend, a poet and scholar, and also a professional healer who was trained to listen to people with problems like mine.

That morning it was the teacher in Gary that shone brightest. He suggested the grant be used as a sort of springboard. "I'll call several friends," he told me, "people who not only want to learn but will also come back and use the knowledge they gain to teach others." He assured me he could get a group together in time for a trip during his upcoming summer vacation.

My mind was on Gary as I sat in a conference room looking out at a redwood forest. He had just confirmed by telephone that a total of five psychologists and doctors would be in our group, people who not only wanted to learn from the shamans but were also in positions to help others.

Ecuador seemed far away from the retreat in northern California where I was attending a meeting of the board of directors of an organization called Katalysis: North/South Development Partnerships. The president of our Honduran partner was speaking in Spanish. Above her voice, I could hear the wind in the redwoods. The beautiful sound, like a chant from the plant kingdom, transported me to those other giants, the high canopy trees of the rain forest. I realized that it was not so far after all, that I would be back in the Andes and Amazon within two months.

I wondered about the persons in Gary's group and their capacity to learn from the shamans. The trip would last only eight days. Would they be overwhelmed? Three specialized in drug and alcohol rehabilitation. How would they react to the psychotropic plants, like ayahuasca, that the Shuar were sure to offer?

The president of the Honduran organization ended her discussion with an announcement that we would take a short coffee break. I hurried outside.

As I wandered through the redwoods, I noticed the similarities between them and the high canopy trees. Both struggled valiantly to reach the sun; the ones that made it were tall, straight, and elegant, testaments to the power of the seed and perseverance.

I saw a lone figure standing under one of the trees and recognized it as Candelaria, the head of a Mayan cooperative in Guatemala. She was a strikingly beautiful woman whom I had met briefly the night before at dinner. Then, as now, she wore the traditional embroidered blouse and long skirt of her people. She turned to me. As she did so, a bell tingled in the distance, summoning us back to the meeting.

"A wonderful place," she said, coming up to me.

I asked whether she had been to California before.

She laughed. "No." She told me it was the first time she had ever traveled outside Guatemala. We walked along in silence. The wind sang in the trees above. I asked her how she liked the United States.

"All my life," she said, "I've heard so much about your country." She paused for several minutes as if lost in contemplation. "It is very different," she said at last, "from what I had expected."

"In what way?"

She explained that the buildings were bigger, the stores more opulent, that there were many more cars and greater material wealth than anything she could possibly have imagined. Then she gave me a strange look. "But something is missing," she said with an odd sort of smile. When I pressed her, she had difficulty describing it. "A feeling," she said, adding, "I don't know exactly, but I find myself asking questions like, Where are the smiling faces? Where are the laughing children working side by side with their mothers and fathers?"

"With all this wealth," I coached, "you would expect to see more happiness."

She nodded. After pondering for a moment, she said, "Yet this wealth you have here is only an illusion. My people have a saying that a person's value is measured not by the amount of corn in his fields but by the sunshine in his heart. True wealth has nothing to do with buildings, stores, and cars." We were joined by several other board members, and together we all returned to the conference room.

We were a large gathering, representatives from the boards of five nonprofit organizations—two from Guatemala, one from Honduras, one from Belize, and one from the United States—all joined together in a close partnership to help low-income people achieve economic self-sufficiency through environmentally sustainable means. I was one of the newest members, this being only my second board meeting, and I was highly impressed by the unity of philosophy and purpose I had seen so far. The sole sticky issue seemed to be the one that was absorbing most of our time this particular morning.

The Central American partners were concerned that the North American partner had no U.S. clients. As one of the Belizeans put it: "You serve us very effectively, providing management services, advice, and fundraising capabilities, but until you offer ways for us to help your people—for southerners to assist our northern brothers and sisters—you will not be a true partner."

The concept that the development process was a two-way bridge was a relatively novel one; the question of what assistance southerners could provide to northerners generated lively discussions. There was little precedence for this type of debate, and we continually got bogged down in philosophical asides that—I thought—reflected individual biases (and northern arrogance). It began to appear that the discussion would take up the entire day, jeopardizing our moving forward with the agenda in a spirit of partnership.

Then Candelaria requested the floor. This was her first board meeting; she was newer even than I was. She began by introducing herself as representing a cooperative composed of 280 Mayan groups.

"We Mayans know a basic truth." She held up three fingers and described how all life rested on three pillars: mineral, plant, and animal. "All are equal, all have spirit. All are one." She emphasized that humans are merely a small part of one of the pillars. Her speech, her very presence, left no doubt that in her view our species did not hold any exalted position; we were not enthroned at the top of some hierarchical pyramid. Then she raised her other hand above the fingers and drew an imaginary arc in the air. "Over all," she said, "is the universe. And below"—she lowered her hand to form a plane beneath its mate—"is Mother Earth." She took a breath and glanced around the room.

I looked from one to another of my fellow board members, especially the North Americans. Everyone's attention was riveted on Candelaria. My eyes met hers and I thought I detected a twinkle. "Mother Earth is sacred," she said, "as are each of the pillars and the universe. We humans must always protect what is sacred." She paused, staring down into her own hands. Then, again, her eyes traveled the room. "Maybe that is why we are here. Perhaps it is this basic truth that we in the South must teach to you in the North."

When she sat down, no one spoke. I realized then that I should not worry about how the group Gary had assembled would react to the Shuar—the message itself would take care of that. All I needed to do was to get people there, to make it possible for more of my people—the northerners—to come in contact with the Candelarias and Numis of the world.

Candelaria's speech was transforming. Aside from the effect it had on individuals, like me, it resulted in a new way of looking at the world for Katalysis. We had been involved in developing training centers in Central America to teach local peasant farmers more efficient techniques for farming, based on sustainable, organic approaches. Following Candelaria's impassioned remarks, someone suggested that the training centers include a place where tourists from the United States and other countries could learn about sustainable farming. This quickly expanded into a concept that included teaching tourists about shamanism, mythology, renewable energy, and holistic medicine.

Within the period of a year, Katalysis would apply for a two-and-a-half-million-dollar grant to develop training centers not only in Central America but also in—of all places—Ecuador. A key component of these centers would be a place where northerners could learn from southerners (primarily indigenous peoples) about honoring Mother Earth, about the unity of all things, about the sacredness of the three pillars, about dreaming a new dream.

During that same period I would lead three groups into the Andes and Amazon, a total of thirty-five people. It would begin with Gary's trip and then expand. Within a year and a half it would include a program for twelve students who would spend five weeks studying among the Quechua and Shuar to earn nine college credits—and gain a wisdom never before imparted by a fully accredited U.S. college curriculum. For all of the forty-seven people, it would be a transforming experience.

5

Into Ecuador

It did not take me long to realize that the people who joined me on the trips were going to exerience something that would turn their perceptions of life upside down. Traveling from the United States into the high Andes and deep Amazon to work with shamans was a journey not only through space but also into other worlds and times and deep into each individual's soul; it was an adventure in self-discovery, a challenge to remold one's way of thinking, feeling, and living.

The volcanoes themselves, the indigenous people and their villages, the rain forests, are all so distant from the lives we are accustomed to that they seem at times not to be real, or at least not part of the world in which we northerners live. Words such as *awe-inspiring, magnificient,* even *sacred* are inadequate to describe both the places and the responses of the travelers to them.

Understanding the importance of preparing people for these experiences, I first encouraged them to attend one of my workshops. Then I made it mandatory for them to participate in a workshop at Miami International Airport before departing. Throughout our time in Ecuador, we worked together as a group, in small teams, and one-on-one; we held discussions, psychonavigated, and practiced several forms of shamanic journeying and healing. My objective always was the same: to have the participants experience their oneness. I wanted them not just to talk about the unity of all things but to feel it deep inside with such intensity that it would forever change their dreams. I hoped that when they returned home they would continue to be aware of their absolute unity with those mountains, jungles, people, plants, animals, and minerals, and know that everything they came in contact with would feel it too; every single thing and every single person, I hoped, would become more attuned to the sacredness that surrounds and inhabits us.

In the following pages I have tried to convey some of that feeling, tried not so much to describe what happened and was said as to capture the intensity and sensuality of the experiences.

"We live in parallel worlds," I told the group of men and women who would accompany me on this trip to Ecuador. We sat in a circle on the carpeted floor of a room on the eighth floor of the Miami Airport Hotel. "You will see this clearly once we reach the Andes. Most tourists visit only one world. They see the material poverty of the indigenous people, the adobe homes, the dirt floors, the lack of cars, toilets, electricity, and all our other modern conveniences. Depending on the quality of the tour and their guides, they may get a glimpse of the closeness these people share with Pachamama, Mother Earth; but they do not see the parallel worlds. They do not gain a feeling for the intense spirituality of the Quechua-speaking peoples—the Cotopaxi, Colorado, Cañari, Otavalan, and Salasacan communities—or of the Amazonian tribes like the Shuar, Huaorani, and Lowland Quichua. They do not come to understand that Pachamama is everything and that these people are in many ways far wealthier than we are."

I explained that Quechua was the language of the Incas; that its various dialects are spoken by people ranging from southern Colombia to northern Chile; and that it, not Spanish, is the dominant language in Ecuador, Peru, and parts of Bolivia. "Quechua speakers represent many cultures that were conquered and incorporated into the Incan Empire. To this day, many have retained their ancient traditions. They do not see time and space the same way we do. They believe that everything that ever happened or will happen—in our concept—is still happening. It is all running along in parallel."

Even though the men and women in the group had been educated to believe in a different set of philosophies, they seemed to accept and understand this new idea. "The shamans we will work with are able to access these parallel worlds in order to obtain knowledge. They may use what they learn to diagnose illness, to heal, or to cause other changes."

"They psychonavigate," someone commented.

I could not suppress a chuckle. "That term is very much favored these days. By definition, *to psychonavigate* means 'to travel through the psyche to a place where you need to be'. For the word *psyche,* you can substitute *subconscious,* Jung's *collective unconscious,* or *parallel worlds.* And the 'place where you need to be' can be a physical location, such as a new campsite if you are a nomad. Or it can be a place where you find answers to questions, an emotional, intellectual, or psychological state, the type of place artists, poets, and inventors journey to."

One of the women asked, "What does it mean 'to travel'?"

I explained that in my experience there were an infinite variety of ways to travel. "It is really a matter of accessing those other regions, the parallel worlds. Some cultures, like the Shuar, use psychotropic plants; others rely on drums, smoke, fasting, sweat lodges, ceremonial dancing, prayer, or meditation. I really believe that the most important thing is intent."

"So anyone can be a shaman."

By way of responding to this, I told them about my friend Raul, an Ecuadoran who would meet us that evening at the Quito airport and accompany us during our travels throughout his country. "Raul was educated in U.S. schools. And he has studied shamanism among many Quechua speakers as well as with the Shuar. He is convinced that the only way to restore the balance between humans and nature is for us in the North to embrace shamanism. We must all recognize the tremendous power within us and use it in positive ways."

"But I still don't understand how it works," someone pressed. "From a scientific perspective, how do you explain and verify this business of traveling to parallel worlds?"

I answered by trying to describe my own psychonavigational experiences. "When I journey," I concluded, "I am truly there. I feel, smell, hear, even taste—and of course see—the place I go to. I know that I can come out of it at any time, come back to this world, but while I am there I am truly there, with all my senses. As I see it, that is a meaningful test. Scientists rely on their senses to substantiate the results of their experiments. So do shamans."

I summarized a few of the many "miracles" psychologists, medical doctors, and I had witnessed: people on previous trips cured by shamans of backaches, tumors, chronic fatigue syndrome, intestinal disorders, and migraines, as well as obsessions and other overtly psychological problems. I admitted that I had found no completely satisfactory explanation of how it works. "There are many theories," I said, "ranging from that of quantum physics, where the healing is attributed to the 'observer effect' and subatomic vibrational patterns, to the more biologically based idea that it is connected to cellular memory and DNA."

"I guess it isn't all that different from modern medicine," another man said. "We take a lot of pills and drugs because they seem to work. Yet we have no explanation of how or why they cure us."

"Sounds to me like science fiction," another woman volunteered. "Time travel. It sounds as though you're saying that shamans have the ability to travel backward into the past and forward to the future."

I explained my own theory, that it was a journey not so much forward or backward but rather to another simultaneous event. "It is all happening right now. In the shaman's view there is no time outside the present."

A man with a beard, who had watched us all very closely but had remained silent until now, cleared his throat. "Einstein," he said slowly, "predicted this. He theorized that if we could travel faster than the speed of light we would observe the past and future happening concurrently with the present."

"We know that if we lived on a planet a hundred light years away," a woman next to him observed, "and had a powerful enough telescope, we could watch our great-grandparents in the 1890s." She glanced around at her fellow travelers. "Doesn't that support the shamanic view?"

The room was quiet. I gave them a few moments with their thoughts before speaking. "During the next few days," I said at last, "you are going to see and experience incredible things. Some of you will be cured of pains and illnesses that have defied modern Western medicine." I paused and watched their intent faces. "I look forward to hearing your theories during the flight back next week."

After flying across the top of the jungle in a single-engine plane that does not seem much larger than some of the birds skimming along the tree-tops below, the people who travel with me into Shuar territory are confronted by the Suntai River.

FIGURE 7   River in Shuar territory

Photo by Ehud C. Sperling

It is the sort of river that in much of the world would be classified as "dangerous" and would be challenged by experts in the most advanced rubber rafts available. But the Shuar lack these; instead they use canoes that have been dug out of huge tree trunks. Never having seen a safety harness or government regulation, they navigate through the fierce rapids with long poles, one man standing in the bow, another in the stern. Although they enjoy a sense of balance rivaling that of the monkeys who often come down to the shoreline to cheer them on, they are nevertheless intimately familiar with the bruises and broken bones that may result from being hurled into the river when the dugout strikes a submerged rock while hurtling through the snarling current.

I had seen the river many times, and always the sight was unexpected. The beach where the canoes were hauled had been as wide as a six-lane turnpike at times, and at others as narrow as a jungle trail. The water could rise twenty feet in less than an hour after a good rain. There had been times when I was sorely tempted to race back to the landing strip before the plane could leave and demand that it return me to the snowfields of the Andes.

But I had never witnessed anything like the sight that confronted me one day in late August. Because of the size of the group, we had formed three teams for the flight; I had led the first planeload, while Raul stayed back with the others. Upon landing, my group had gone immediately to the Suntai. We found a raging beast that had devoured the beach. Its waters had overflowed the banks and, like a dragon's angry tail, lashed through the trees at the end of the path. I stood there in awe.

Then it occurred to me that this was a sign, and perhaps a blessing in disguise. Among our group there had been a great deal of worry over the issue of ayahuasca. After learning that the Shuar shamans would make it available, people had been torn. Most of the eleven were psychologists; a couple were medical doctors; one was a business executive with a strong interest in using psychonavigation for stress management. Intrigued as they were by the idea of taking a plant substance that was reputed to have the power of transporting the user to other realms of reality, they nevertheless labored and argued over the decision of whether or not to participate. I had worried that the issue might divide the group and, in an effort to defuse the topic, had made it clear that ayahuasca was not part of the program and that, although I myself might risk drinking it, I recommended against its use.

Now, it seemed, the entire issue had been resolved by the Suntai.

I turned to one of our Shuar guides. "Mati," I said, feeling both a sense of relief and disappointment over the prospect of missing the jungle experience, "clearly we can go no farther. We should take the plane back before the rain socks us in."

He threw his head back and laughed. He turned to his Shuar companions and described the Suntai as a castrated lizard. Their laughter joined his. Then, pointing at three dugouts tied to trees along the bank, he said to me, "We take canoes to Numi."

His confidence shattered my resolve, but I wasn't about to be taken so lightly. "I've visited you many times, but I've never seen it close to this high," I protested.

Although he agreed that it was unusual, he insisted that we take the canoes, assuring me that the current was not dangerous. "The rains stopped last night." He strolled confidently to a nearby tree and placed his hand on a watermark even with his chest. "Tsúnkqui's anger has passed," he said, adding with a smile something about not finding a Shuar within miles of a canoe if Tsúnkqui were still enraged. Then he turned abruptly away and, along with his companions, began loading our supplies into the canoes.

Before long they were helping us climb in. None of the others spoke Spanish, but several in the group wanted to know whether what we were about to do was dangerous. I could only tell them that the Shuar did not think so. In response to one of their questions, I asked Mati how many Shuar had been lost to the river.

"Lost?" he replied. "We are never lost when on the Suntai, only sometimes in the forest." All the Shuar found this comment to be uproariously funny.

We headed into the river; each of the canoes had a Shuar standing at the bow and stern. Almost immediately we felt ourselves being sucked along by the hissing current.

I had to fight a sudden wave of nausea. I must be crazy, I thought, to bring people to this place where life was so full of risks. The image of the shaman's lodge and the haunting music of an ayahuasca ceremony flashed before me. I knew I must rid my thoughts of all negativity. The world is as you dream it, John. I forced myself to concentrate on the rain forests that lined the sides of the river.

The area we traveled through, on the eastern slopes of the Cutucú Mountains, was rugged, not the flat tropical plain that comes to mind when most people think of the Amazon basin. At times the tributaries feeding the Suntai drop from cliffs right out of Edgar Rice Burroughs's Lost World. The animals that inhabit this region, the plants, insects, and reptiles, are also different. Some are not found anywhere else on the planet. We were passing close to the home of the hoatzin, a creature that is believed to be the evolutionary link between bird and reptile. As I forced my mind to focus on these things, my stomach began to settle. The people accompanying me had come on this journey to learn about the power of the seed, the empathetic unity shared by all, the dream. I thought about Candelaria's three pillars and knew that I had many lessons to learn.

The canoe lurched violently to the left. I grasped the gunwales with both hands. We struck a rock. Shouts rang out. The warrior in our bow jumped into the river. Wedging himself between the rock and canoe, he used his legs to push us out into the current, then quickly vaulted back in. Ice-cold water splashed over my hands and cascaded into my lap.

We shot into a swirling maze of rapids. I stole a glance at the faces around me. Every member of our group looked terrified. The Shuar, on the other hand, appeared to be enjoying this mad ride. Directly behind me, Mati, our helmsman, was concentrating intently on the task at hand, yet he had about him an air of bemused detachment. For a brief second his eyes met mine. He smiled.

Suddenly the excitement was over. We drifted casually along a peaceful stream. Parrots squawked in the surrounding forests. Susan, who sat in front of me, turned to face me. "That was the scariest thing I've ever done." she said. "But isn't it wonderful to be alive!"

I recalled the words to a Shuar male initiation song: "I was born to die fighting." I turned and asked Mati if those words were truly sung.

"Oh yes," he said. Then he laughed. "But of course we don't believe in death, not the way you Christians do." I thought about Tsúnkqui, Núnkui, Ayumpum, and all the other gods who walk among the Shuar.

I looked into the forests along the banks of the Suntai with a new awareness. Here were places where spirits not only tread but are acknowledged. Part of the allure of ayahuasca is its power to put the user in direct contact with the spirit world. The Shuar knew there was a risk involved, yet the risk was well worth taking.

Risk. The word had a whole new meaning when uttered within the context of these jungles and the people who populated them. For most tribal people, the risk was not so much one of dying but of not living properly. It was the quality of your time on Earth, not the quantity, that was important. How different that dream from the one I had been taught!

Where, I wondered, did we get the idea that we must do everything possible to postpone the inevitable? Why do we put such stock in the notion that progress is established by increasing life expectancy statistics? What is it about the words *more* and *longer* that has made them assume such a paramount position in our language?

I thought about this as we traveled on, deeper and deeper into the rain forest. I realized that the farther we went, the greater became the risk of dying. There was no doubt that if a canoe capsized or someone stepped on a poisonous snake or had an attack of appendicitis, it would be next to impossible to get him or her back up the river, to the airstrip, and out to a hospital. The farther in we proceeded, the greater the probability that any accident would result in serious injury or death. At first I felt this as a gnawing ache in the pit of my stomach, accompanied by the now-familiar thought that I must be crazy to bring people here, to take on not only the personal risks to my own life but also the risks of lawsuits and other liabilities. But then, as I watched the trees on the riverbanks and listened to the birds, as I looked about at the faces of the people who had come together here representing so many different backgrounds and felt the cold sting of the water on my face and hands, a strange thing occurred.

Glancing up, I saw a pair of soaring birds in the azure sky. As if choreographed by some providential power, they pirouetted in a dance that seemed intended to speak directly to me about the need to free myself from my material fears. Those fears, now irrelevant, were replaced by a feeling of liberation. With soaring heart I became one with those birds, with the forests, the sky, the river, and one with all those other spirits that were represented by the faces in the canoes. Moments from the past, dreams, and memories of times when I had followed my heart, all of these came together for one instant, and I felt them crystalize within my heart like a brilliant and multifaceted diamond I would wear forever.

People often fall in love on my trips. Perhaps this is because of the country itself. From the snow-capped Andes to the steaming rain forests, Ecuador is charged with sensuous energy. One hour you are awed by the incredible majesty of the world's highest active volcano; the next you are standing astride the equator watching a snow blizzard engulf gigantic Cayambe; then you drive past fiery Sangay and suddenly find yourself in the heart of the Amazon jungle, drinking chicha, a fermented drink made of manioc root, with a shaman who has taken heads and is an expert on psychotropic plants. Or perhaps it is the Indians themselves, their exotic clothes, mysticism, erotic music, their love for Pachamama, their children, their animals, the way they honor life and glorify death.

It is, I suspect, these and more: the bombardment of scents and sounds, of marketplace herbs and flutes playing tunes in scales unfamiliar to northern ears; the taste of naranjilla and other fruits too delicate to export; the feel of a blanket woven from alpaca wool; and the sun in the thin air at seventeen thousand feet beating down on shoulders chilled by twenty-degree Farenheit winds. Most of all, though, I believe people fall in love on these trips because they begin to accept the idea of an empathetic unity, which is central to the indigenous philosophy. They feel at one with each other and the world around them.

The love transcends the experience. It stays with the travelers for a long time, perhaps forever. When they return to their homes in the United States or Europe, they want desperately to stay in touch—both with each other and with Ecuador. They set up networks and newsletters and organize reunions. Many return to Ecuador. This type of love expresses itself in a thousand ways. While it is always sensuous, it is more likely to be platonic than sexual. It is always deep and passionate—and it is confusing because it is so different from what we are trained to feel.

I felt this love for Alice Fieldstone, a Los Angeles cardiologist, one night as we stood side by side listening to a shaman named Yampun describe the ayahuasca vine. Illuminated by the glow of his fire, he held before him a piece of gnarled wood that looked like a root. His fingers appeared barely to touch it, and his voice was hushed. Kitiar, the Shuar elder whom Yampun was assisting, stood reverently next to him, watching with great interest the expressions on our faces as we listened.

Suddenly there was a commotion outside. Yampun exchanged words with a woman whom we could not see. Kitiar went to the doorway and spoke into the night. An elderly woman and two younger men entered. After a brief greeting, she held out a finger for Yampun to inspect.

I felt Alice inch away from me so she could get a closer look at the finger. "Bad infection," she whispered. She slipped off into the shadows.

Yampun examined the finger and then carefully studied the woman. He turned to Kitiar and spoke in Shuar. While they were talking, Alice returned. In her hand, held discreetly out of the Shuars' sight, I glimpsed a small tube of ointment.

Yampun's wife, Secha, arrived. After a brief discussion, she led the woman with the infected finger outside. Kitiar signaled for the rest of us to follow. In the darkness we groped our way along a jungle path, until finally we came to a.stop. Secha was standing next to a tree. She held a lighted candle and something that occasionally glittered like a firefly.

I could hear a voice chanting, but could not tell whose it was or even whether it came from our small group. Secha moved her candle up the trunk of the tree. She placed the glittering object against the bark and I saw that it was a small knife. Slowly, meticulously, she cut a tiny groove and with her blade collected a ball of sap. Without hesitation, she applied it directly to the woman's wound. After that, she lowered her candle to knee level and rummaged in the bushes that bordered the path. She broke off a leaf and carefully laid it over the sap-covered injury.

"Will it work?" I asked Alice as we headed back down the dark trail.

"I have no doubt it will. These people know what they're doing." She reminded me that many of the drugs prescribed in the United States originate in the rain forest, and added, "Imagine how being cured directly by a tree affects your outlook! The intimacy shared between people and nature here is wonderful."

Instead of returning with the others to Yampun's lodge, we walked to the river, where we had a clear view of the starlit night.

"Makes you wonder," she said, gazing into the heavens, "where it all began and how we got to where we are today." She told me about a college professor who had impressed her with his theory of evolution. "He shook up the place because he insisted that choice—not mutation and natural selection—is the key."

As she related it, the theory sounded a lot like Numi's assertion that everything is molded by our dreams. She used the example of the evolutionary link between the deer and moose. They both descended from a common ancestor. "But," she said, smiling gently, "somewhere along the route, one decided to run from a saber-toothed tiger while the other stood and fought. The first visualized itself flying like a bird away from its enemy, the second saw itself as the victor in a heroic battle."

I felt very close to this doctor from Los Angeles as we lingered there next to the river in the middle of the jungle and together shared the stars and a theory about the way life on our planet had developed. I found myself wrapping an arm about her shoulders. She leaned into me and gave a little shiver.

I began to talk about an idea I had been struggling with, and how although the idea appealed to my heart, I had difficulty reconciling it with my scientific education. "We believe we reached some pinnacle of intelligence during the last several hundred years that allowed us to invent steam engines, power plants, airplanes, and computers." But this belief seemed ridiculous. "Does it imply that our brains suddenly grew?"

"Medical science would laugh at that suggestion."

"Then what is the explanation? Are we to believe that the Mayas, with a mathematical knowledge that allowed them to design a calendar more accurate than our own, could not produce weapons any more advanced than stone maces? We know that the Chinese had gunpowder long before Europeans, yet used it only for celebrations. Can we possibly believe that it took some superior creativity that existed only in Europe to understand gunpowder's potential in war?"

She squeezed my hand. "It was choice."

"It had to be." We walked on, with an arm around each other. It was the first time I had shared these ideas with another person. I told her that I had concluded that since combustion engines and electric generating plants are powered by fuels that can be obtained only by mining Mother Earth, that dream was rejected by our ancestors as a nightmare.

She protested that the ancient Greeks, Egyptians, Romans, Indians, and Chinese had done their share of mining. "All that marble, all the armor." She expanded this to include the Aztecs and the Mayas themselves.

I agreed, but pointed out that it had been done within strict limits and always under divine guidance. "Every one of those civilizations saw themselves as servants of a greater power." We stopped and, as if by common signal, stared up into the stars. "The Shuar, too, mine in their own way. They harvest salt and manioc, palms for their houses, ayahuasca from the forests. But they always ask permission first and, afterward, give thanks to Núnkui or one of their gods."

"So intent makes the difference?"

"Not so much the intent as the dream. At some point we changed the dream from an Earth-honoring one to an Earth-dominating one. It may have been a result of the Black Death, which killed off so much of the world's population back in the fourteenth century. In Europe and Asia, where the plague spread, people's fear of nature's immense power provoked a need to control nature, a quest to dominate it so that a catastrophe of that magnitude could never happen again. Before the Black Death, people sought answers from the Church; afterward, they sought them from science. The technologies of mass pollution became possible."

A bend in the river had turned us back in the direction of the lodge. Once again under the trees, the light of the stars had been replaced by the faint glow of candles ahead.

"The deer and the moose," she said. "Earth-honoring civilizations and Earth-dominating ones." Her voice went silent. We walked on until we reached the circle of light where she brought us to a stop. "Yes, I think I see a connection." We turned from the light and peered into the forest. Fireflies flitted about the vague outlines of giant trees, lending the place a mystical quality. The ancient sound of a wooden flute drifted out of the lodge.

Her body moved in front of mine. "I just decided to take the ayahuasca," she said.

I took the chill that ran down my spine to be a premonition. "Perhaps you shouldn't." I was frightened for her.

"Yes." From the way she said it, I knew she had made up her mind. "The plants have things to tell us. The least I can do is listen."

She threw her arms around my neck and, pulling my head to hers, kissed me. We held each other close for a long, precious moment. Then she broke away and, like a beautiful moth, flew into the light.

We stood with our Shuar friends in the dark jungle clearing under the stars. We whispered, like worshipers in a cathedral, sensing that those distant worlds might hear and be disturbed by our voices. Earlier, a storm of meteors had illuminated the sky with such brilliance that one of us had wondered aloud whether it was a hail of burning arrows, an attack from a neighboring tribe. Now we all looked to the west at a flaring light in the distant darkness. It distinguished itself from the stars not only because it appeared to be so much larger, more intense, and obviously much closer, but also because of its color, a deep red glow that gave it the appearance of a bloody wound hacked through the armor of night by some gigantic and violent enemy.

It was Sangay, the immense and very active volcano that, for many Indians, has the powers of a sacred being. We could see only its fiery summit but knew that the massive mountain was beneath, reaching upward from the jungle floor on the outermost fringes of the eastern Andes into the blackness above. It was reputed to be perfectly conical in shape, but few could verify this, for during the daytime it remained shrouded in Amazonian mists, a mystery even to those who lived in its shadow. Many claimed they could always feel it throbbing, like a mighty heart, beneath their feet, and hear its constant rumble; yet seldom did they see it. To them, it was a constant presence, but—like a god—one rarely encountered in its physical manifestation.

Each of us knew that, in witnessing Sangay's explosive dance, we were receiving a rare gift. We North American pilgrims, huddled there among our Shuar teachers, gave thanks to the spirits of the jungle for their generosity. One of us said it was an omen; another that it was a torch beckoning us to lead our own people out of our materialistic plight. Somebody compared it to the Star of Bethlehem.

As I watched that mighty volcano erupting into the star-filled night, I came to understand what the Quechua mean when they say that Pachamama is our true mother, that the woman from whose womb we are born is just a surrogate—a person to be loved and respected, yet only a vessel for Mother Earth. I felt my kinship to this passionate and sometimes violent parent who provides everything I need, the food and water, air and fire, my clothes and shelter. I realized that when the Otavalans talk about being liberated from their human mother's womb so they can return to Earth, they are speaking literally.

I thought back to a time when all had been eruption, when every rock was molten lava and boiling plasma flowed like oceans across our planet's surface. Great clouds of vapor enveloped every inch. Complex chemicals swirled about, their atoms performing ritualistic dances that through the mysterious alchemy of creation resulted in life. A time of violent birth, a time when any witness would have seen in Pachamama absolute proof of a living, creating, sentient being.

I realized too how much more difficult it is for us to see such proof in hardened rocks, the fossilized remains of that great burst of procreative activity. We sometimes feel it in the winds, smell it in the forests, and hear it when surf breaks along a craggy shore, but those are only hints, mere symbols, of the pulsating planet that lies beneath us. It takes the violence of a hurricane, the destructive ripping apart of continental shelves in an earthquake, or the frenzy of a tornado to wake us up. And yet even then, we awaken only partially. When the passion ends, we slip back; we modify our zoning laws, strengthen building codes, and convince ourselves that we are omnipotent rulers.

But not here, not in Ecuador, neither in the Andean domain of snow-capped volcanoes nor in the steaming jungles of the Amazon Basin, for here we feel the power, cannot help but sense the energy of our breathing, still-creating Pachamama. We become aware of our own frailty, our dependence on her for sustenance. As we stood beneath the stars watching Sangay explode, that relationship seemed so very obvious.

The next morning we hiked to the thermal falls. As we picked our way along the slippery river rocks and up cascading currents of icy water, everything around seemed to echo the message of the fiery volcano: *the Earth is alive*. I could hear it in the roar of the rapids, smell it as I passed the lush arrays of hanging orchids, feel it while wading chest-deep in the glacier-fed river as the tropical sun beat down on my shoulders, taste it in the vines and bark our Shuar guides offered when they stopped to explain the uses of a plant, and see it in the profusion of species that walked, crawled, flew, and grew in every imaginable configuration. I felt it in the cliff we had to scale, and was thankful to the rock for each toehold it offered.

FIGURE 8   Thermal falls, Shuar territory

The three waterfalls at the thermal falls cascade through a veil of mists down to the gorge below, which has been carved into the rock by the river we had hiked along for most of the morning. Only two of the falls are actually thermal; they are steaming hot, born in a volcanic womb deep inside Pachamama. The third is ice-cold. Unlike its sisters, its birthplace is the snowfields at the top of the Andes.

"Here," one of our Shuar guides said, pointing excitedly, "is where the mountain spirits meet the cave spirits."

At the bottom of each fall is a deep pool that is ideal for swimming. Close to the thermal falls, the water is almost boiling, but as you drift away it turns increasingly cooler and more bearable. The pools for the glacier-fed fall and one of the volcanic falls have merged. You can stand on a ledge in the middle of this combined pool and, stretching out your arms, feel the hot, steaming spray in one hand and the frigid, glacial waters in the other. I have stood there and felt those waters many times, overwhelmed by the simple knowledge that I am part of the Earth's magnificent diversity.

We took off our clothes and plunged into the water. We—Shuar and North American alike—were children at play, screaming into the air and splashing each other. Even the most reserved members of our group frolicked with an abandon that had been foreign to them for perhaps decades.

Michele, a doctor from Chicago, swam over to me. "If everyone could spend a day the way we've spent this one," she said, "no one would bulldoze another forest." She glanced around, then back at me. "Can't you just feel the intelligence of this place?"

Now that I looked—truly looked, not just with my eyes, but with all my senses—seeing life in all that surrounded me was not so difficult. Walking back from the themal falls, I recalled how the Quechua talk with rocks. When a loved one is far away, they send messages to each other through the Earth. A woman may sing a song to a stone. It is passed along to the next stone and on and on until it reaches her lover. He hears her song and sends his own message back in the same way.

I stopped in the middle of the river and, reaching down, ran my hand along the surface of a rock. It was sleek and wet, yet at the top it was warmed by the sun. I spoke to it, asking it to let my wife and daughter know that I was thinking of them. Then, involuntarily, I glanced sheepishly about to see whether anyone was watching.

I walked on and laughed aloud at my own embarrassment. Why are we so convinced that we can send messages through copper wires and fibers, but not through the rocks such things are made from? I thought again of Sangay and the molten lava that once flowed across all of Pachamama. The knowledge that we all emerged from that—every one of us, stone and tree, reptile and rodent, flower and human being—was taking on a new and profound significance for me. Did it not mean that we are indeed all one, in the most literal and practical sense?

Then suddenly I was back at a much earlier time, transported to the very beginning, to the eruption when it all began, to the birth of galaxies. I recalled the beautiful descriptions of that moment by the mathematician Brian Swimme and the philosopher Thomas Berry in their book *The Universe Story*: "If in the future, stars would blaze and lizards would blink in their light, these actions would be powered by the same numinous energy that flared forth at the dawn of time."* It was a moment of absolute energy and power, yet rather than being an explosion, it was an unfolding, a gift that sprang from a single all-encompassing space and time like a sprout from a seed. And from that moment every creation that was ever to follow was conceived. We all originated there, all of us together, each one with the others, from a single source, united in the collective dream of the one space-time seed of originating power.

---

*Brain Swimme and Thomas Berry, *The Universe Story: From the Primordial Flaring Forth to the Ecozoic Era: A Celebration of the Unfolding of the Cosmos* (San Francisco: Harper San Francisco, 1992), p.17.

6

Ayahuasca

"Do the Shuar still shrink heads?"

A group of us were lying in the hammocks, our heads pointing toward the central pole. Rain fell heavily around us. It poured off the low-hung thatched roof with the force of a waterfall. We were eight in all, seven North Americans and Kitiar, a Shuar elder who, even among other shamans, was recognized as a man of special powers and ancient knowledge. The crackling fire sent smoke curling into the rafters. Shadows danced up the walls and into the thatch, where they united with the smoke.

After hearing my translation, Kitiar answered that very few heads were shrunk these days. "And," he added, "the jungle has suffered." He turned in his hammock, dangled his feet over the side, and explained that in the old days a man had shrunk heads in order to gain power. Killing, he told us, was a necessary part of initiation into manhood. "To create life, you first must take life." Now, he said, babies were conceived even though no death occurred; the balance was gone and the fragile jungle was being overpopulated.

I could see from their expressions that what Kitiar said shocked some of my friends. "My God," one of them muttered, "another unforeseen result of the missionaries' zeal."

"You mean to say, head-hunting was really a virtue?" another asked incredulously. "Why and how did they shrink them?"

When he heard this question, Kitiar's wrinkled face broke into a broad smile. He fairly leaped out of his hammock. Although perhaps close to eighty years old, he was still spry and vigorous, his body firm and athletic. "We shrunk the heads of our enemies," he said, "so their vengeful souls would stay inside and not come after us or our families." He followed up by using his own hands and head to demonstrate the process, showing how a cut was made around the shoulders and then up the back of the head so the skull could be removed. The fleshy mass was dropped into steaming water. After a few hours, the mouth and other openings were sewn up to assure that the vengeful spirit could not escape. Kitiar went to the fire; kneeling before it and using a small gourd to demonstrate, he told us that for several days the head would be filled with sand that had been heated in the fire. The shrinking process continued. The hot sand and also small stones were used to mold the head to its original—although much smaller—shape. Holding the gourd high, he ran his fingers over it to illustrate the ways a shrunken head might be painted to look more realistic.

"Sounds like he's experienced," one of the listeners observed. "Has he taken heads?"

Kitiar rocked back onto his heels. He held his palms open to the fire. In its glow, his cheeks looked sunken; every wrinkle created a shadow. His dark eyes were clear and luminous; they were ancient eyes, eyes that pre-dated written history and spoke of courage, strength, and compassion. He watched the smoke as it bathed his hands and rose into the darkness of the rafters. He nodded slowly. "Many," he said. "But long ago."

"Where are they? Can we see them?"

I explained that Kitiar kept them hidden away in a safe place, adding, "Although he now attends Sunday mass, he still believes the vengeful spirits will kill him and his loved ones if they escape."

Kitiar stood up, and as he did so his arms encircled the smoke, sweeping it into his body. "The spirits are all around us," he said slowly. "In the jungle. In this lodge." He walked over to the wall and peered through the palm staves and the rain into the forest.

Ann rolled out of her hammock and went to stand beside him. "I wish I could speak your language. Your view of life is beautiful." I translated.

He turned to her. "Life," he said, "is beautiful. But death is even more beautiful, because it allows us to realize our destiny."

She glanced around the room at her companions, then spoke directly to Kitiar. "I can't disagree with you, but you must know that such a concept is difficult for gringos to understand."

He nodded and smiled. "I know that." He returned to the fire. "I know also that you came here so you could understand it."

Taking the cue from him, she squatted next to the fire and waved the smoke into her.

"See," he said. "Already you have learned to bring the spirits to you."

Shortly after Kitiar left, the rain ceased. We lay in our hammocks listening to the sounds: the fire crackling; a couple of chickens pecking a path around the hard-packed dirt floor; a pig squealing contentedly in the mud outside; birds chirping; the cicadalike buzz of a rain forest insect.

"This whole idea of dreaming the world," Jerry said, "sounded very intellectual back in the States. You know, 'the world is as you dream it' and all that. But now I think I begin to see the point."

"These people really live their dreams," someone added.

"Isn't that what ayahuasca is all about?"

What followed was a long discussion about the "vine of the soul." It was an opportunity I had been awaiting because, although I had made it very clear that ayahuasca could be deadly and that if people took it they did so against my recommendations, I suspected that several in this group would partake. It was therefore important that they learn as much about it beforehand as I could teach them. I told them that it was a serious—and painful—event, that they should fast for at least twenty-four hours before drinking it, that ayahuasca was an obnoxiously bitter toxic that would probably cause them to vomit violently and perhaps defecate uncontrollably within an hour or two after consuming it. I looked around at the bodies lying in the hammocks.

"So what's the bad side?" a woman's voice asked sarcastically.

"Other than the possibility of receiving a Shuar burial?" a man piped in. "Do we get our heads shrunk?" Nervous laughter bounced around the room.

"That's about it," I said.

"And the good side?"

I watched the shadows play in the thatching over our heads. For a moment I was transported back in time to my own first ayahuasca experience. I could smell the terribly sour liquid that made me gag as it went down. I could hear the melodic music, feel myself being pulled away into a world of bright colors, talking plants, and multifaceted geometric symbols.

The sound of someone's voice asking me to tell them more brought me back to the present. It was not a discussion I wanted to have, but I knew I owed it to them. I tried to be objective, tried not to romantize or bring any of my personal biases into play. I drew on descriptions I had read and heard from others as much as memory would permit. I told them that a good ayahuasca journey would take them deep into other worlds, where they would find it easy to communicate with plants, animals, and the Earth herself.

I discussed how strong messages I had received after taking ayahuasca had resulted in major life changes. I also told them that I had gained similar insights while psychonavigating without ayahuasca or any other substance, that a good psychonavigational journey was very similar to an ayahuasca trip, although shorter and less intense—and safe. I also emphasized that, according to Shuar tradition, a person should not discuss his or her ayahuasca experience with anyone other than a shaman, at least not until several weeks had elapsed. In former days, part of the initiation into manhood included a trek to the sacred waterfall; once there, the initiate had taken ayahuasca, performed a ceremonial "dance" with the waterfall, and received a vision that often included a verbal message from a voice booming out of the jungle. The initiate then would be filled with incredible strength, both spiritual and physical. On the night before attacking his enemy, he shared his vision and message with his comrades—to do so earlier would result in a loss of power. If his vision had been a true one, he would be victorious the following morning and would return to his family with the head of his enemy.

"How will it differ from the psychonavigation workshops you give?" Peter asked.

I remembered the workshop he had attended several months before at the University of Pennsylvania. There had been capacity crowds—nearly two hundred for the evening seminar and full-day workshop combined. "You'll have a lot more room for spreading out." I laughed. "The classroom will be a real shaman's lodge; it won't have concrete walls. Nobody threw up during my workshop—at least not that I'm aware of." Looking at him, I realized the question deserved a serious answer. "I really can't say, Peter, except to tell you that this is dangerous, that was not."

"And this is a once-in-a-lifetime experience that has been described by some very intelligent people as the most extraordinary thing they have ever done."

"All of the above," I agreed.

Ayahuasca became the focus of the group's attention. It was our second day in the Amazon, and no one seemed interested in a prolonged conversation about anything else. Individuals wandered about, observing the jungle, listening to and looking for birds and butterflies; they swam in the river and talked with the Shuar. But whenever members of this group of medical doctors and psychologists got together, the conversation inevitably turned to ayahuasca.

Seven highly educated, middle-aged professionals, all extremely well trained in one or more aspects of Western medicine, all very experienced, respected, affluent people to whom others turned for help with their problems, several of them specialists in drug and alcohol rehabilitation—and to a person they were obsessed with ayahuasca. Why?

I did not feel that I could ask them this question, not now while they were contemplating taking it, but I did ask Numi, who lived in the village where we were staying. I found him sitting on a log down beside the river. Since that day when I had first met him on the beach, eighteen months earlier, he had taken a bad fall that had caused severe arthritic pain in his left leg. Physically it had slowed him down, but his eyes remained young and alert. Nothing about his intellect or his intuitive wisdom had slowed in the least.

"Everyone is always intrigued by magic," he replied with a twinkle in his eye.

"Ayahuasca is magic?"

He gave me a quizzical look. "Wouldn't you call something that allows you to travel to other worlds magic? Or that makes it possible to call wild jaguars and anacondas to your side? To chat with plants?"

This did not satisfy me. "Well, then," he said, "if not magic, ayahuasca may fascinate us because of its sex."

"Sex?"

He explained that it accomplished what even sex was incapable of doing. "When we make love, we try to unite with the other, we try to unite also with our own parents, but we fail. Only through ayahuasca do we succeed. And our experience is forever. Once we have been there, we never forget."

I asked how he, a former teacher at a Catholic mission school, could believe such things. He looked shocked. "But it is completely consistent." Christ, he said, gave us bread and wine to draw us together as one and the same with him and God. "As tribes throughout the Amazon know, we were given ayahuasca to sanctify our unity with the forests."

We sat there in silence for a while, watching the water that had been born in high mountain glaciers glide past on its way to the mighty Amazon. He stood up and massaged his lame leg. Then he asked whether I knew the nickname for ayahuasca.

"Yes," I said. "Vine of the soul."

He laughed. "That is one of them. Vine of death is another." It was the first time I had heard that name. I must have given a start, for he stepped close to me and touched my elbow in a reassuring gesture. "The way we say it, you see, they are one and the same."

"The soul and death?"

"Of course. When we die our soul is released; it is one with all else, the universal dreaming! Again, as Christ teaches."

We walked together along the bank of the river. He moved carefully, and I could tell that the exercise pained him. "You see," he said, "the Shuar and Christians—true Christians—believe the same thing. We are all connected, all brothers and sisters in the deepest possible sense, because we are the same, hatched from a common egg"—he spread his arms—"we humans and everything we see, everything we touch, smell, hear, taste, and feel with our sixth sense. We have the same mother. Christ knew that." He pointed up to the tops of the trees that lined the river. "Look there. The jungle has many levels. The high canopy where the harpy eagle lives. On down. The toucan level, monkey level, sloth level. This one where we stand. And below, the snake level, root level, birth-of-waters level, fire level, and so on."

He stopped and turned to face me squarely. "Most important of all is the spirit level." He made a motion with his hands around his body similar to what Kitiar had done while kneeling before the fire. "They are here with us all the time. We know them through our dreaming. We can feel them, as Jesus Christ did, but sometimes it is difficult to see them when we are not dreaming. Ayahuasca helps us." He patted my shoulder. "That is what I call magic. And it is a type of magic you in the North have lost—most of you, anyway." He chuckled. "But perhaps 'sex' is a better word. I think maybe your people can relate more to the idea of impotence in sex than loss of magic."

A thought occurred, which I shared with him. "The Lakota people in North America have a sun dance; it puts the dancers into a trance that they compare with being dead." I described in as much detail as I could remember how after regaining consciousness the participants tell of a peaceful world where they visited ancestors and other guides of great power and compassion. They are left with a profound euphoria and a conviction that they have joined a universal whole. From this experience comes a short prayer that is often quoted ritualistically by the Lakota: "I am related to everything that is."

He clasped his hands together. "That is wonderful!" He bowed solemnly. "So very Shuar. So very Christian. You people should take that to heart and make that prayer a part of all your rituals."

I had to confess that my people had outlawed the sun dance about a hundred years ago. "I've heard," I added quickly, "that it is now making a comeback."

We continued walking in silence. A butterfly fluttered by and landed on a stone near the water's edge. Numi squatted next to it. He studied it intently. The thought crossed my mind that perhaps he saw the soul of a loved one in it. "Wonderful markings," he observed as he stood up. "They resemble a mask. See how obvious that butterfly is out here on this rock. But in the jungle it becomes invisible. Like the spirits!"

As we walked on I told him about psychonavigation, explaining that I had found it to be very similar to the ayahuasca journey, but without the physical discomforts or dangers. He said that the Shuar are familiar with such techniques. "In fact, they are practiced all the time. A good shaman lives on other levels more than on this one that most of your people call the 'real' or 'ordinary' one."

"Then why bother with ayahuasca? Why take the risk?"

"There is risk to everything we do on this plane. Walking along this path. Eating food. That is part of being alive. But the worst that can ever happen is that you move to another plane. I said 'worst,' but in both the Shuar and true Christian perspective that is in fact the goal." He chuckled at my obvious confusion. "As for ayahuasca, it is a way to take communion, like Christ's wine. It is an offering from the plant level." He described the shaman as being a human agent of change and ayahuasca as the plant equivalent. "Some people are content to sit in meditation and gain peace of mind. Not the shaman. He or she must create change and teach others. Some plants are content to be, but not ayahuasca. It must create change, teach. That is why shamans and ayahuasca work so closely together. This is true of people throughout the rain forests, from the Andes all the way to the Atlantic Ocean."

We arrived at the place where the river is squeezed between two rock walls. We had to scramble up the slope in order to continue along the trail. This proved to be an effort for Numi. His leg was a burden. When we reached the top, he was gasping for breath, but a pleased expression lit his face.

"If only I were a true believer," he said, "I could have dreamed myself up here."

"Like Christ walking on water," I joked, catching myself too late.

He gave me a hard look. "Exactly," he said slowly. "Yes, exactly. I have always taken those things literally. I know many of my brothers in the church do not. Perhaps it is my Indian background. The shamans, of course, the really powerful ones, have always done things the rest of us think of as miracles."

"How?"

"They dream it. What we dream, happens."

The shaman's lodge was dark. Night sounds from the jungle filtered through the walls. We five gringos who would take ayahuasca huddled together in a corner, trying to cope with our fear. We had fasted for twenty-four hours, yet at that moment none of us could have eaten.

We watched our comrades seated around the low-burning fire. They ate catfish that had been netted from the river by our host's son earlier in the afternoon and manioc roots, which resembled long, stringy potatoes. Occasionally someone would speak in a hushed voice, but otherwise the lodge was still, as though we were attending a funeral rather than a celebration of our oneness with all the entities in the world we inhabit.

A light moved through the darkness toward us. It was Chankín, the shaman's daughter. In the candle's glow I could see the face of the baby she carried wrapped snugly in a shawl around her shoulders. The baby's face shone out from the dark cloth. Chankín offered a calabash of chicha to Jan, the person in our group nearest her. I watched Jan look across the lodge to Raul. As ever, he was alert to everything. He nodded. "It is good to drink a little," he said softly.

I thought about the horrified reactions these people had shown back in the Miami airport when I had told them that the most important component of the Shuar diet was a beer made by chewing and spitting manioc.

Yet now, five days later, they drank it with relish, commenting on its uniquely fresh flavor. They had indeed come a long way.

I lifted the calabash to my lips. The cool chicha brought a vision of the health food store near my home where we bought kefir, a slightly sour liquid yogurt. I handed it back to Chankín and she moved on to Alice, sitting next to me. I closed my eyes. I tried to focus on the smells and sounds of the health food store, tried to close out those of the lodge, the Shuar family, and the jungle around us. I wanted desperately to forget my fear.

But it did not work. My thoughts kept returning to the ayahuasca. I wondered whether I would have trouble vomiting or whether instead I might be wracked with diarrhea. I worried about passing out and never regaining consciousness. I wondered why I had decided to do this and then realized that such fears, although normal for someone about to take ayahuasca, would infuse me with negative energy and that if they persisted I would have to decline the cup as it was handed to me. I saw myself standing before the shaman, refusing the offering in his outstretched hands. I felt humiliated.

Then he was there before me, holding a candle next to his bare chest so that the dark tattoos that dotted his cheeks and nose were illuminated. His voice was a low chant. On his head he wore a crown of macaw feathers—black, gold, and blue with tips of red that shot like flames into the night. His muscled thighs gleamed in the firelight as he kneeled in front of me and touched a finger to my forehead. Something cool and sticky followed his finger down between my eyes and drew a bridge across my nose. He moved slowly, with care and delicacy. His concentration never appeared to falter. He spoke softly, words I could not understand, stood, and moved on to the person at my right.

I looked left and saw that the three before me had been painted with bright red markings. The designs were simple lines along the forehead and around the nose, yet somehow—perhaps because of their simplicity—they were elegant, sacred.

He finished and faded into the shadows at the end of the room.

Our companions had moved back from the fire that now was reduced to a faint glow of embers. They, like we, were totally silent. The only sounds were those from the jungle, the croak of tree frogs, the high-pitched wail of a night bird, and an occasional scream that I took to be that of a distant jaguar. Wind swept through the trees like the whisper of lost souls.

Then the music started, almost imperceptible at first. The soft sound of the tumank, a stringed bow that is held in the mouth and plucked with a finger and that sounds like a mouth harp but much gentler, as though played by heavenly angels. After a while it was joined by a wooden flute. The melody seemed to come not from one area of the lodge but from all around, as if the forest itself were vibrating the tune through its leaves and bark. As the volume slowly increased, the instruments were joined by a man's voice chanting. Yet it too seemed a part of the forest, not anchored but drifting, an echo that filtered through the palm walls of the lodge and wandered about among the trees and animals of the night.

A tiny light flashed at the far end of the lodge and settled down into the flickering glow of a candle.

A shadow towered above us and spoke in Raul's voice. Jan rose and followed it to the tiny light. The music ceased.

There was the soft hum of Shuar voices. I knew Jan must be drinking ayahuasca. I realized that I was no longer fearful. The softness of the night, the way the shaman had painted us, his very presence, all these had calmed me. A shudder of anticipation and perhaps relief went through me, but now that I knew I would go through with it, I also understood that this night would offer things not seen or felt before.

Jan returned. "Foulest stuff I've ever tasted," she said, laughing, and sat down. Raul's shadow reappeared and motioned for the person on Jan's left to follow.

Finally it was my turn. I approached slowly. The shaman was an apparition sitting on the floor. Only his feathered crown caught the candle's light. I stood before him very still. He spoke several words and handed me a gourd cup filled with an orange liquid. I said a brief prayer. I held the cup out, bowed to him, and drank it in a single gulp. I had to fight back the urge to spit. The toxic vine was bitter beyond belief. Raul handed me a bottle of trago. "Drink, brother," he said. "Just enough to wash away the taste." The burning cane alcohol did the trick. I thanked Raul, bowed again to the shaman, and walked over to one of the "beds," a platform made of split palm staves large enough for several adults to stretch out on.

I lay there looking into the thatch above. The music resumed. This time it was the two-stringed violin. A vision appeared of the shaman making it, patiently carving away on a single block of wood with a machete. The violin emerged out of the wood, and I watched him lift it to his chin to play.

My stomach began to gurgle. I could feel the ayahuasca inside and, closing my eyes, saw my intestines. A stream of orange fluid flowed through them. I felt myself being lifted by the music and carried down an orange river. The tempo increased and I picked up speed. My intestines were pink and purple and I sped through them at a dizzing pace. I felt mildly nauseated. Opening my eyes, I saw Karen standing above me.

She sat down next to me and began to massage my chest. "How do you feel?" she asked.

"Wonderful." I wanted to tell her that she should have taken it also, but decided not to. "I think I'm in heaven," I said. The music wound down.

In the background, I heard the squeal of guinea pigs. "Guinea pig heaven." We both laughed uproarously. She stroked my arms and shoulders, but I could not stop laughing.

Raul's voice emerged from my laughter. "Slowly, brother," he said. I felt his hand on my chest. His face was close to mine. He spoke in a whisper. "Focus. You have much to learn here tonight. Concentrate on vomiting."

As both he and Karen moved away, the sound of the tumank drifted over me. I was flying above ancient cities. I was a gigantic bird soaring over Incan, Mayan, and Aztec monuments. They were decorated with brilliantly colored patterns. Beyond them was jungle. I thought about vomiting. A Mayan pyramid erupted in an explosion of orange liquid that filled the sky. I started to rise, but knew that it was premature. I concentrated on my stomach and began to worry that I might not vomit at all. The thought occurred that the poison might linger there for the remainder of my life. I suddenly felt very cold. I wished I had not taken the ayahuasca.

I stood up, reeling with dizziness. Karen was suddenly beside me asking what I wanted. I explained that I was cold. She helped me lie back down and covered me with a blanket. I closed my eyes. The ancient cities reappeared. The violin became a tumank, and my flight changed with its rhythm.

I descended into the cities and sped down mazelike passages. On either side, huge temples rose into an azure sky. The passages were lined with giant masks that watched me as I flew past.

I became aware that someone was outside vomiting. He or she—I tried but could not determine which—seemed very close, right next to the wall beside me. It was a terribly painful, wrenching sound, as though the body were regurgitating itself. I decided that perhaps I did not wish to vomit after all. I recalled hearing someplace that not everyone needed to vomit. I felt comforted. A movement in the thatching above caught my eye.

At first they were mere shadows. Then slowly, they emerged as a pair of snakes. Before my eyes they grew. They uncoiled endlessly, reaching several times the length of a man. Their eyes were like burning embers. They appeared to be copulating. I felt drawn to them. I rose to a sitting position and found that the dizziness had subsided. One of the snakes swung down from a rafter, enticing me to join it.

Suddenly a person rushed past me. Then another. They went outside. There was a commotion, voices raised. The music stopped. Raul stood in the doorway, a body in his arms. He moved quickly, carrying it to where the shaman sat chanting in a low voice.

Panic burst through me. The ayahuasca had killed one of my group— and I was responsible! I started to rise, but was pushed back down by a gentle hand. "Relax, John." It was the voice of Rosa, a Shuar woman who spoke Spanish.

"What happened?" I demanded, pointing at the body now lying on the ground near the shaman. "Who is it?"

"Relax, John. It is the doctor woman." Grief overwhelmed me. Alice Fieldstone had died. I began to cry. Rosa hugged me, mumbling words of assurance. "*Esta volando*," she said. "She is flying."

Immediately I saw Alice's soul flying above us, struggling to free itself of earthly bounds. I had a desperate urge to pull it back, until I looked into the eyes and saw something there that put me at ease. She was at peace, and her peace filled me with a feeling of tranquillity.

"I'm all right," I said, and stood up. Rosa did not try to dissuade me this time. I made my way to where Alice's body lay. Raul was kneeling at her head, as though in prayer. The shaman bent over her. He lifted her blouse and placed his mouth on her stomach. Then he began sucking.

He made loud, violent sounds. I watched her soul hovering above, resisting his efforts to retrieve it. I wanted to cry but, looking into those eyes, found I could not. The shaman straightened, leaned to the side, and vomited.

I discovered that I was back on my own bed. Rosa stood up and moved away. Alice's soul turned from me and I closed my eyes. The ancient cities returned, but now the sky was dark and menacing. I began to fly down the corridors. The temples around me sprouted arms. The masks grimaced. The arms tried to grab me. I picked up speed, but tentacles stretched out and plucked me from my journey. Suddenly, I was above the corridors, hurtling through space. A moment's relief gave way to a vision of what was below: a land flowing in blood and dotted with severed heads and leering death masks. It was beyond my endurance. I opened my eyes. I heard someone regurgitating. A great wave of nausea rushed through the lodge.

I stood up and headed for the door. I was sobbing uncontrollably. A voice kept shouting at me. "You must throw up," it screamed. "You must empty yourself of the deadly poison, the wretched ayahuasca snake."

Outside, I immediately fell to my knees and tried to vomit. Great wrenching spasms of nausea undulated up from my intestines, but nothing came out. I was wracked with dry heaves, excruciatingly painful and frightening.

A hand steadied my forehead and another pressed against the back of my head. "Concentrate, John. Vomit," Raul's voice said.

But I could not. I looked up into his eyes. "Alice?"

"Flying," he said. "You mustn't worry about her. Focus on your own journey. Vomit. Alice is in another land."

"I can't vomit," I said, and rose. My pants were covered with mud. Alice's soul flew off toward a distant star. It grew smaller and smaller until finally it disappeared. I thought I heard her voice.

Raul helped me lie down on my bed. "Focus," he said. Through my closed eyelids, I saw him return to the place where he and the shaman had worked on Alice. The violin music resumed. It seemed faraway and sad. Alice was lying in the hammock, back where we had been before all this began, beckoning to me. "I love you," I said, "but I'm not ready to join you. Why don't you come back?" She smiled sweetly. She shook her head. "You must vomit," she said.

A group of people huddled in the corner. From the way they gestured, I could tell they were agitated. They moved toward me as one. They made an angry, buzzing noise, like bees defending a queen. They shook their fists. One of them stepped forward and announced that they were Alice's family. They would, he told me, destroy me and my family. They would send me to prison and make life miserable for my wife and daughter. "I have to vomit," I said, struggling to a sitting postion.

Feeling miserably sorry for myself, I sat there. Then, as if the roof had suddenly flown off the lodge, a great light flooded the room. I lay down. Strength rushed into me. The light was a lake of energy; it fed a mighty river that poured power into me. I felt myself grow. I knew what I must do. I would walk out of the jungle. In no time at all I would reach a radio and call in a U.S. Air Force helicopter. It would take Alice back to a hospital in Miami and cure her. I got up.

I was taller than the tallest tree. My head rose through the top of the lodge. The stars shone on me. Then I realized the folly of my plan. No U.S. doctor could cure Alice. I sat back down and pulled my body inside itself, to its normal size. I knew that Alice was in the best hands possible.

I walked through the door into the night air. My head was clear. I could see as though the sun were shining. Someone was sitting on a rock off to the side. I could not believe my eyes. "Alice?"

She turned to me. Her hand reached out.

"You're alive!" Our hands connected. Hers was warm.

"Of course," she said. "But I still haven't vomited."

I threw my arms around her. I felt ecstatic. "I thought you were dead."

"I'm very much alive. I've been flying."

"I love you," I said. I thought about that word, *flying*; it suddenly took on new meanings. Then, feeling that she needed to be alone, I wandered away. I felt so relieved, so grateful, so euphoric, that I kneeled in the mud and silently shouted my thanks to God, Jesus Christ, and the jungle.

A leafy branch reached out to me. It was phosphorescent. I touched it and as I did so heard it speak.

"Silly—you thought *flying* meant death. You let the negative rule you. It is a pattern in your life. Let this experience with Alice teach you a lesson. Purge the negatives."

I began to cry. I crawled through the mud to the trunk of the tree and hugged it. I felt indebted to this plant for the wisdom it had imparted. I cried into its bark, thanking it with all my heart, knowing that it was right and that I would always remember this lesson. I thought about vomiting and, even as I did so, realized that this was just another negative. I had let the fear of not vomiting control me. Like my attitude toward Alice, it had been allowed to dominate, to sap my energy and detract from the special experience of this night. No longer!

Slowly I rose to my feet. I stepped into the jungle; mud seeped over my boot tops. I could glimpse my friend Gary by the lodge, sending me a vibration to let me know he would be there if I needed him but would not intrude. The smell of foliage and organic mud moved in on me and covered me like a blanket. It was so intense that I could feel and see it, gray and warm and welcoming. I knelt in the mud and opened my hands at my sides. The energy of the forest pulsated into me. It flowed with a rhythm, like that of a drum, vibrating down from the canopy, through the trees and bushes, picking up power as it came and piercing me. I could see myself kneeling there, hands outstretched, head lifted to the treetops, could look down as though from a branch and watch the shafts of light flow into me, shimmering waves of energy that encircled my body like spears and sent power into my every pore.

Pure joy, euphoria. I felt completely at one with the forest, the mud, and the night around me. I could see deep into the Earth herself, could feel energy pulsating up from layers and layers of shimmering minerals, could hear the magma bubbling, smell the molten lava, taste the greenness of life, and could at the same time hear the song of distant stars, as though the universe outside and inside the Earth were connected in some way that I had never before imagined but that now seemed obvious and practical and so very much a part of me.

A wind sighed through the trees. "Asssk," it said.

"What must I do?"

There was a long silence. All the energy that had flowed into me, the smells, sounds, sights, tastes, and feelings, came together into a ball surrounding my heart. I looked down and saw myself kneeling in the forest. The ball expanded out through my chest. Crystal clear and pulsating with light, it grew and grew until it enveloped me. It lifted me up out of the mud, up into the tree, where I united with myself.

"Save us," the wind said.

The trees bowed. "Save us," they repeated.

"I will try," I promised. I hugged the tree and then flew like a silent owl down to where Gary was standing.

He embraced me. And I knew that he wanted to return to the lodge to listen to the shaman's music.

The music was wonderful that night. Not long after returning to the lodge, I felt the ayahuasca surge up into my throat. I rushed outside and vomited. The night became peaceful and beautiful. The shaman and his family chanted, sang, and played their instruments until first light. I drifted in and out of various levels of reality that were totally separate from our normal perceptions of time and space. I became aware that I could travel through many universes simultaneously. It was not so much that these were parallel universes as that they were all one, and I was in and of that oneness in a way that allowed me to experience everything. The barriers we erect, the compartments we build around time and space, became meaningless. I did not tear them down; I simply understood that they do not exist except as words that mold our perceptions and, in the process, take on an energy that can, if allowed, control our actions.

Many months after that night, Alice told me that the shaman had sucked the ayahuasca out of her. He had described this—through an interpreter—as "reducing the potency." She had been unconscious, she said, when Raul carried her into the lodge. She recalled feeling weak as she stood in the clearing. Her knees buckled. Then memory ceased until she found herslf lying on the dirt floor. The shaman was sucking on her stomach and vomiting. Very quickly after that, she regained her strength. At first she had still believed that she needed to vomit, but soon after I had discovered her sitting outside on a rock, she realized that the ayahuasca had been removed by the shaman. She never did vomit, nor did she suffer any ill effects.

She also told me that the shaman had asked what else needed healing. For several years she had suffered from severe migraines and mentioned this to him. He immediately went to work sucking and massaging her. She has not had a migraine since.

Then Alice made a remarkable confession. She believed that she might actually have been dead during the time between when her knees buckled and the shaman revived her. She has no recollection of what it was like, only that, "looking back, I feel that I was dead." Coming from a rather conservative medical doctor, a member of the American Medical Association who has been practicing medicine in the United States for over twenty years, this struck me at the time as an extraordinary statement. It still does.

7

A Personal Journey

Several months later I returned to Ecuador with another group. That trip turned out to be especially powerful for me, owing in large part to the work I did one night with Kitiar. I believe that what I experienced that night is worth describing; not only does my personal journey provide insight into the ways the shamans work, but—perhaps more important—it shows us how we can alter our dreams to create a more Earth-honoring society, re-define our relationships with the nonmaterial world, and redirect our ener-gies toward a better balance between people and nature.

Four of us had decided to take ayahuasca. While the others ate dinner, we prepared ourselves by drumming and chanting in the lodge where the ceremony would take place. One of us, a young musician, had brought a battery-powered electric guitar that he had had specially made so that it could be disassembled and carried in a backpack. He and the two women had attended my workshops back in the States; a bonding had occurred then, and we now felt privileged to be sharing this night with each other.

Lying in hammocks near the fire, we looked out into the rain forest night. The guitar sang eerie melodies that formed a bridge between the steel-and-computer world whence we came and this vine-and-earth one that sur-rounded us and filled our senses.

I reached over and took Samantha's hand and felt her hammock swing as she took Lydia's. Jim's hands were busy on the guitar. I thought about the parallel worlds I so often discussed, then, realizing the futility of merely thinking about them, felt them intuitively. Those worlds were surrounding me, penetrating me; they were part of me. "All one," I said.

"Ain't that the truth," a woman's voice responded.

The sound of her words jolted me. I felt a moment's panic as I realized that I was about to take the vine of death again. I thought about Alice and wondered how many people had died from ayahuasca, or simply not re-turned. Who needs it? I wondered, then answered the question myself: no one. But I have a job to accomplish. I knew that sharing this ceremony, this plant, with Kitiar would help me. It was worth the risk.

Kitiar arrived. We stood to shake his hand. His energy electrified me. I had not remembered it being so strong. As we returned to the hammocks, he began playing his mouth bow, the tumank. The other participants filtered slowly into the lodge. Kitiar's music brought magic. The Shuar say it calls in the spirits who are the oneness. I could feel their presence, our presence, in the music, the crackle of the fire, the air, and stars. Kitiar invited Jim's guitar and my drum to join his tumank.

Then he stopped. The only sounds were those made by the millions of spirits who serenade the forests every night. His chanting began, and one by one, each of us four was called up to take the ayahuasca.

It was thick and bitter. I knew immediately that Kitiar had given me a highly concentrated dose. Raul was standing near. He handed me a bottle of trago. Although I sipped it, the bitter taste lingered.

When I returned to my hammock, I felt mildly apprehensive. But there was no turning back. I looked out under the leaves of our roof at a giant palm silhouetted against the starlit sky. It beckoned me up, away from this world of worries, into one of a higher consciousness. I felt myself relax. The tranquillity of the night enveloped me like a soft blanket.

I saw Kitiar's face up there in the stars. The blue-black dots tattooed across his nose reminded me of his ancient past. Back in the late 1950s when I was studying with Mrs. Simpson, he was already in his forties, a mighty warrior shaman who had taken the heads of fierce enemies. I realized as I watched his face smile down from the sky that his spirit was timeless. Even his material world was incomprehensible to most of the people in mine—a swirl of colored photos, reams of anthropological explanations. Yet he and I also shared a commonality. In a very real sense, he, the photographers, the anthropologists, and I share everything. We share it with the engineers and construction workers who pave over the forests as well as with the white-frocked scientists who debunk shamanic healing. We all live in parallel worlds on many levels, All of us are one, united by our dreams. All of us are as ancient as Kitiar.

The sound of a wooden flute drifted into my consciousness. Kitiar had set aside the tumank and taken up the flute. I rode its notes up to the top of the palm. The stars spun around me. I looked down at the ground and into the lodge where the ayahuasca ceremony was in progress. I felt dizzy. Bile rose from my stomach to my mouth. I rolled off the palm and found myself staggering out the door of the lodge. I retched, but was able to produce only a dribble of bile.

I sat on a log. A hand touched my shoulder. "Are you okay, John?"

"Just fine." I looked into Raul's soft eyes. "Can't quite vomit yet."

"You will," he said, sitting down next to me. "It is a beautiful evening. Full moon."

His eyes were focused on the sky behind my head. Dizzy, I tried to turn, but it took an incredible effort. Moving my head was a monumental task. At last I saw the moon, bright and full and encased in a shining white ring. The sight took my breath away. "My," I said, "how very sacred."

"Yes," Raul agreed. "A special night for ayahuasca. Another special night for you."

I raised my hands to solicit the power of the moon. "Help me, Mama Kilya," I pleaded. "Help me vomit and get on with what I must accomplish."

Immediately I began vomiting violently. Raul helped me lean forward. He held my head the way my mother had when I was sick as a child. I had fasted for over twenty-four hours and was shocked by the volume of what came up.

"Pure ayahuasca," Raul said reassuringly. "You'll feel better soon."

The vomiting turned to diarrhea. Raul, like an angel of mercy, comforted me. He told me that the power of my purging would be reflected in the journey I would take. After what seemed like hours of agony, he helped me walk back to the lodge. I kept thinking about death. I knew that part of me had died and that now the vine of the soul would take over. I felt relieved, but at the same time exhausted and dizzy. Raul seemed to understand exactly how I felt. He guided me with great tenderness and compassion. Later I would realize that an eternal bond was forged between us that night. He led me to a bench and helped me lie down. Nan came over with a bottle of water and held my head as I sipped. Having been with me and taken ayahuasca herself on a previous trip, she understood what I was experiencing.

Raul, Nan, and I chatted softly for a time. I drank more water and munched on a cracker. Then Rosa, the Shuar woman who had helped me when I thought Alice had died, approached us. "Kitiar is satisfied that John has purged himself well," she said. She touched my shoulder. "Come to him now."

Once again Raul assisted me. We walked across the lodge and I lay down on a platform near Kitiar. The shaman was once again playing his tumank. Then he was standing silently above me, the fire behind him. From my perspective, lying there below him on the bench, he looked gigantic. Through Rosa, he asked what I needed.

I summarized the earlier experience with him and ayahuasca, my dialogue with the jungle and my commitment to save it. Then I explained that, although I had made progress, I felt that I had recently encountered a barrier. "I don't know what it is," I confessed. "Lack of direction or courage, or perhaps I need more patience and creativity. It puzzles me. All I know is that I've come up against an obstacle. I feel that I need your help."

Without a word, he began chanting. He bent over me and shook branches of leaves above my body. I felt a wind blow through me. The leaves brushed across my face, down my chest and arms, along my stomach and groin, and out over my legs and feet. As they passed above my toes I felt the wind again, as though it were sucking something out of me and transporting it away, through the bottoms of my feet. At the same time, I had the distinct sensation that I was rising slowly above the bench and was suspended there in midair. The sensation seemed totally natural at the time, not in the least bit threatening or unusual.

When he stopped I found that my eyes had been closed. I recall no vision, just the feeling of levitation. I opened them and saw Kitiar sitting on a stool beside Rosa. The two of them had a very long conversation in Shuar. After they had finished, Rosa turned to me. "He has cleared the barrier," she said. "You can go forward with your mission now. Seek guidance from your inner pilots, ask questions, and move down the path without fear." She paused. He said something. "Yes, without fear. That is very important." She stopped.

"That's all he said?" I asked, remembering the length of their discussion.

"Yes. Isn't it enough?"

I realized that my question sounded impertinent. "The message, yes. I will take it to heart. It's just that you and he had such a long conversation. . . ."

She chuckled. "The problem of languages. Shuar is much richer than Spanish in such matters." She spoke to Kitiar and they both had a good laugh. Then he stood up and walked to the fire, mumbling something as he walked away. "Ask questions," she said, then went to join him.

Raul accompanied me to my hammock. I lay down, closed my eyes, and immediately saw geometric figures and long winding passageways. I traveled down one of them and came to a closed door, heavy and ominous. When I asked it to open, it laughed at me. So I shot backward out of the passageway and tried a different one. It led me to another door, less threatening in appearance; this door opened.

I found myself in a small room. On the floor was a tiny bulldozer made of plastic Lego blocks. As I stood there, it grew to become suddenly large and lifelike, no longer a toy. Its engine started with a roar. It drove directly toward me and then, at the last moment, swerved to avoid hitting me. Instead, it rammed the wall behind me. To my surprise, the wall did not crumble—it simply moved back. The bulldozer pushed it far away, to the edge of the horizon. The other walls stretched with it in a way that left me standing in a long, narrow room.

The bulldozer raced back to me. It turned and struck one of the side walls, pushing it like the other to the horizon. It repeated this process with the remaining two walls. I was now standing in a huge room, whose walls formed the horizon. The bulldozer had vanished. Recalling Rosa's words, I asked, "What was that all about?"

My question had barely been asked when I heard a deep, clear voice. "Your world must push back its walls. Help your people, your culture; extend their limits of understanding. The arrogance of your culture has trapped you all in a prison. Push outward. Extend wisdom. Move into new patterns of thinking that are not confined by the walls of recent history."

The vision faded, and I was now traveling down another passageway. I tried to concentrate on the message I had received, but another voice told me to let it go. "You will remember," it assured me. I shot up out of the passageway into the sky.

A flock of what I took for birds flew high above, mere specks in the clouds. I heard a dull roaring sound. They descended toward me. Amazed, I saw that they were airplanes. In the front were the Wright brothers. After them came sleeker biplanes, followed by World War II–vintage models, then the big four-engine prop planes, and finally, modern jets. They engulfed me, deafening me with the sound of their engines, each group louder than the one before. The winds they generated were terrifying in their power.

As suddenly as they had appeared, they were gone. There was no voice to explain them. I felt that I would come to understand their meaning later.

I opened my eyes, suddenly aware that Kitiar had been playing his violin and now had stopped. The lodge was dark except for a single pinprick of light, which I thought must be coming from a candle near where the shaman sat. Despite the blanket over me, my backside felt cold, and I realized that my hammock was thin. I wished I had my sleeping bag.

I lay quietly looking out through the walls of the lodge, at the top of the palm where I had perched earlier in the evening and at the stars beyond. I felt calm, although chilled. It seemed like hours passed as I waited for the music to resume. After a while I saw a shadow I thought I recognized near the doorway. "Raul?"

The shadow approached my hammock and confirmed that it belonged to Raul. I asked whether there would be more music. "Not tonight, brother," he replied. "Kitiar is flying." He asked how I was doing. When I told him it had been a great night, he patted my knee. "It has only begun," he said. Then he suggested I move to a little room near the lodge where I had left my sleeping bag. "You'll be warmer there and can continue your journey." He helped me up. I was relieved to discover the dizziness had left.

My sleeping bag was warm. It was like a cozy cave, a cocoon or womb. Raul left. I heard rustling sounds in the jungle outside. I was tempted to get up and walk in the forest, as I had that previous time. But another sound caught my attention. The room was buzzing with people. When I concentrated I could see shadows milling about. Straining to focus my attention,

I was able to pick out several individuals, old friends from childhood, high school, and college. The door opened and more came in, clearly now, a parade of people I had known and liked throughout my life. They gave me looks of encouragement; some smiled, others touched me gently. Music played in the background—the tumank. Several of my friends danced to Kitiar's music. After a long and wonderful party, they departed.

The thought occurred to me then that I hadn't asked questions as Kitiar had instructed. I recalled the bulldozer and wondered how I was supposed to push back the limits. Specifically, what must I do?

A huge car whizzed into the room, nearly killing me. Its horn blared a deafening scream. I felt terrified. I was suddenly surrounded by automobiles—black, huge, and ominous. I leaped out of bed and started running, but was blocked by them. Their engines roared at me. I froze. I was pinned in, completely at the mercy of their rage. A voice rose above the horrible racket. "Stop the car," it said.

"No!" I yelled. "I don't want that answer."

"We know, but it is necessary. The car is an enemy to Earth. The metal and plastics. The petroleum."

"But I'm a writer, a teacher," I protested, "not Ralph Nader." The cars came to a stop. I was encircled by them.

"The car is a symbol of materialistic greed and inequality. Defrock the symbol and the disease will be cured. Besides," the voice softened, "you may be surprised. It may not be the way you think. Doing battle with the car could be fun. It will open new doors."

I was standing in front of one of those doors I had seen earlier. It opened to a magnificent sunset that went quickly into night. I stood up. Around me all was black and quiet. I returned to my bed and crawled into my sleeping bag.

I slept. When I awoke I found a package of crackers in my backpack and wandered down by the river to eat them. It seemed to me that another day passed there next to the water. I felt warm, engulfed by the soothing sounds of the bubbling current and surrounded by the forest spirit. Then I returned to my sleeping bag.

I heard music and, looking up, was amazed to find a gorgeous woman dancing naked at my feet. She moved gracefully, sensuously, her beautiful body undulating in a soft light that, I saw, came from candles held by other naked women ringing my sleeping bag. Each was incredibly voluptuous. As the tumank played, each performed a dance at my feet that was completely different from the one before. The women were of the various races, and, I judged, the dances represented cultures from around the world. I was delighted and aroused, but mostly I felt honored by their presence and the wonderful energy they focused on me. I fell asleep to the sounds and smells of their dancing bodies and a feeling that I was bathed in love.

I awoke into the morning's light and stepped outside. The world looked fresh, as though it had been purified by rain, although I was certain there had been none during the night. I felt rejuvenated, like a person who has slept for days instead of only a few hours. I spied Kitiar sitting with Raul in the lodge.

Kitiar picked up his violin and played as I sat down on a stool in front of him. Immediately I was transported to the night before. The bulldozer, the airplanes, my friends, and the cars returned. He lowered the instrument to his lap and beamed across it at me. "What a night," he said in Spanish.

"It was wonderful. How can I thank you?"

Kitiar leaned slowly across the space separating us. He touched a finger to the tattoos decorating his upper cheeks and the bridge of his nose. He nodded slowly. Then, in his broken Spanish, he recited for me everything I had experienced the night before: my ascent into the palm, the geometric figures, the long winding passageways, the doors, the bulldozer pushing back the walls, the birds transforming themselves into airplanes, and all my old friends. "What a lot of wonderful friends," he observed.

"That is *my* journey," I said in absolute amazement.

"Yes." He grinned.

"How did you know?"

"I journeyed with you."

I felt both shocked and honored. "Does that happen often?"

"No. Sometimes. It's very powerful." His smile turned serious. "What about the cars?"

I wondered whether he had ever seen a real car. "I guess I'll have to do something about them."

"Yes. You better." Then the face of this ancient warrior broke into a childish grin. "And the women!" He giggled.

I felt myself blush with embarrassment. But it lasted only a few seconds, for I realized that Kitiar, not I, was the guide. "Yes," I said, and we both laughed. "They were wonderful." He nodded enthusiastically and patted my knee. He stood up, setting the violin down on the bench. He bent to pick up several branches of leaves at his feet. "Thank you," I said.

He gave me a long, serious look. A drum sounded in the distance, indicating that breakfast was ready.

"You're welcome," he said and, turning, walked down to the river. He approached a gnarled old tree and stood before it for a moment or two, as if lost in conversation with it. Then, rising on tiptoes, he placed his branches—the ones he had used in his healings, the ones that had cleared my barrier—among its branches.

He came slowly back to the lodge. With painstaking care, he packed his tumank, violin, and flute into a soft wicker basket. He stroked it tenderly. "We've fasted long enough. Let's find breakfast."

Part ❂ Three

The Old Shaman

Manco was psychonavigating as the gringos walked into his room. Although he continued to travel with Sinchi, he noticed many things about them. They carried cameras. They talked incessantly, although in hushed tones—in deference, he assumed, to Sinchi, whose presence filled the room. They wore the richest, most perfect clothing he had ever seen. About them hovered a smell that was like the soap sold in the Quito market, sweet enough almost to turn his stomach. He held a branch of nettles before his nose and shook it.

Immediately the room went quiet. Outside, the bus gave a final growl and then fell asleep. Manco peered at them through the branch. This was good. He smiled. And every one of them smiled back. He glanced down at the sacred stones lying on the tapestry at his feet, barely able to conceal the relief he felt. Sinchi was making it easy on him. A short chuckle escaped his lips. He looked back at them.

The most amazing thing about these gringos was not their cameras, constant chatter, clothes, or smell. It was their size. Two of the men were giants who, he guessed, weighed at least twice, perhaps three times, as much as his heaviest son. Even the shortest woman among them stood as high as the tallest man in his family.

He picked up one of the sacred stones and moved it in an arc before him. "May you dream of growing smaller," he chanted. "May your childen require less clothing, smaller houses, less food." He stepped toward them. Holding the stone out, he walked slowly down the line of them, passing the stone so close to each that its energy mated with that in their hearts. "May they grow up to be my size and give more than they take from Pachamama."

From the expressions on their faces he knew that not one of them understood a word he said. But it did not matter; the words were not for them. He concentrated on the stone and their hearts. The stone grew cold. He felt its sadness and understood that the physical appearance of these gringos was but a part of another dream. He stopped. He let the hand with the stone drop to his side. It was a dream of bigness, of growth gone beyond the will of Pachamama. His own heart felt heavy. A tear rolled down his cheek.

He lifted the stone to his own heart. It grew warm; he felt strong again. He held it out to them and continued on, remembering that he had never shrunk from a task that Sinchi had given him, recalling how the elder had spoken of being mother and father to a new birth.

At the end of the line, he felt a pull on his chest. At the same time the stone began to vibrate. He stopped before the gringo man and looked up into green eyes that smiled into his. They stood there staring into each others' souls; then Manco turned away and ambled slowly back to the tapestry on the floor.

Deliberately he sat down, motioning for the others to do the same. His hands described a circle, and his guests arranged themselves according to his wishes. He focused on all the huacas, the sacred items in front of him—the stones, freshly cut branches, burning candles, flowers, bottles of fermented sugar cane, fruits, and eggs. He felt the imbalance, not only among the people but also in the alignment of the huacas. A chant rising in his throat, he adjusted them until finally they were balanced.

He stared into the flame of a candle, shutting out all his physical senses, even sight, and was drawn into a journey deep down to the bottom of Cotopaxi. Darkness overwhelmed him. He felt cold, even as he smelled the sulfur and smoke from Pachamama's ancient fires. The taste of ashes purified his internal organs and he felt totally cleansed, inside and out.

A sudden shriek pierced the silence. The mighty wind of beating wings lifted him up out of the crater.

Below him Pachamama was cloaked in dirty fog. An odor, like that of buses on the road to Quito, stung his nostrils. He began to cough uncontrollably. The wings took him higher, into clean air. *Pachamama called out to him. Her voice was a wail; the words were muffled. Strain as he would, he could not understand what it was she asked.*

Then his wings failed. He reeled and began to fall. The wind screamed around him. His body was being torn apart. Down, down he plummeted. The fog around Pachamama opened. He shot through the hole and saw the mountains rising up.

Then everything stopped. The noise, the feeling, the fall. He hovered above his home, the bus parked outside. He was a leaf, drifting slowly down. He heard Sinchi's voice telling him to heal the woman, teach the man. He will become your student.

The leaf slipped through the thatching and came to rest near the sacred stones. The flame danced.

Manco looked out into the faces that looked at him from their circle. "The circle," he said slowly, in the best Spanish he could conjure, "is unity. We are one." He passed his hands over all the sacred items and then held his palms out to the watching faces. "Who will come into this circle to be healed?"

He was not surprised to see all their eyes turn to the man with green eyes. He translated. There was a pause, until green eyes spoke quietly to one of the women. She hesitated, then stood up.

Manco sent a power animal, a llama, to her, then motioned for her to come to him. She stepped into the circle.

"You too, Jungle Eyes," he said to the man, laughing in a way that usually put people at ease with him. "Tell them what I called you."

The man translated. All the gringos laughed along with Manco. He patted the tapestry. "Both of you sit here, in the circle."

After they were settled, he looked directly into the green eyes and again felt a tug in his chest. This was the student Sinchi had referred to, of that he had no doubt.

"This woman," Jungle Eyes began, "has a specific problem. She was diagnosed by a doctor in the United States a week ago. I would like to tell you about it."

Manco held up a hand. "No," he said. "Let me tell her."

8

The Healing

Raul and I had wanted to take the group to Iyarina, an Otavalan shaman in the high Andes who had worked with us previously, but when we arrived at her house, we were told she had stepped out for a few minutes. Her husband encouraged us to wait, insisting that she would return "any minute now." Raul had a strong feeling that we should visit someone else, however, an old man called Manco. I was tired. I liked Iyarina and was inclined to wait. The more we talked about it, the more insistent Raul became. He could not explain why; he said only, "You will see." I had come to know Raul well and to trust him completely, especially when it came to shamans.

Now, as Pauline and I sat in the circle facing Manco, I understood. His power filled the room. I was certain that everyone in the group could feel it. Outside, the Andean night was cold. But inside this man's lodge was an energy that warmed us. Although the only fire came from a candle, people had begun removing sweaters and jackets as soon as they entered. Pauline had requested that I tell him about the tumor on her ovary that a New York gynecologist had discovered seven days earlier; it did not surprise me when he refused to hear the diagnosis.

And there was something else about him. I had felt it when he looked into my eyes, but I could not quite define it. Now, watching him prepare to work with her, seeing the way his arms moved as he touched the stones in front of him and lit a second candle, I kept thinking that I had seen this man before.

He put a bottle of trago to his lips and, tilting his head back, filled his mouth. Then he sprayed a mist across his huacas. Pauline and I got thoroughly drenched. I whispered to her that this was a cleansing, a necessary preliminary to a healing. From her look, I knew that she was having second thoughts.

Manco gave us a big smile as he wiped the trago from his face. He peered directly at her, shook his entire body as if to say, "Horrible stuff, isn't it?" and chuckled in a most engaging way. Her grin told me that he had succeeded in putting her at ease.

Photo by John Perkins

FIGURE 9   A 103-year-old Otavalan Shaman

He shifted his weight to get closer to her. With his left hand he picked up a black-green stone that was shaped like the head of an ancient hatchet. Both hands began to move about her head. Slowly, gently, he seemed to feel her aura.

He whistled a gentle melody as he worked, yet it was obvious that he had entered what we call an altered state. His hands worked their way down her body, caressing the air around her.

When they reached her waist, they slowed. His whistling grew weak. The hands continued to move downward, but with great caution, as though exploring, searching. The right hand began to close.

I glanced at her. She watched him with an intensity I had become accustomed to among gringos studying the phenomenon of shamanic healing, but with her there seemed an added strain, and I sensed the apprehension she had suffered since the appointment with her gynecologist.

His hands stopped. "Here," he said. The expression on her face told me he was right.

He held the stone close to her belly. His right hand knotted into a fist. "There is something here like this," he said. He wiggled the fist.

Her eyes met mine. I started to speak, but was interrupted by his renewed whistling.

Both hands moved in, as though piercing the invisible energy field they had previously respected. I thought she must be able to feel them against her now.

Then he pulled them back.

He looked at me. "How old is she?"

I translated and told him she was thirty.

"Married?"

"No."

He looked into her eyes. "You had an abortion."

I hesitated, reluctant to speak in front of all the others. But she knew. Perhaps it was the Spanish word *aborto*. Her face turned ashen. "No," she said.

He leaned in to her, his face mere inches from hers. "No?" He said it softly, yet left no doubt that he had complete confidence in his art.

She turned to me. She gave a little shrug. "I did have a miscarriage," she confessed. "A couple of months ago."

I started to translate. As I did so, I remembered that in Spanish there is no distinction between the words *miscarriage* and *abortion; aborto* is used to describe them both. I explained that hers had been involuntary.

He nodded. "Of course." Then solemnly he asked, "And the father?"

She glanced down at her hands where they lay folded in her lap.

"You didn't love him," Manco said gently.

Once again, I found it difficult to translate. I felt like an intruder. When I did, her eyes grew moist.

He reached over and touched her temples with his fingers. "You did not want the child. Your energy caused the miscarriage." Haltingly, I told her what he had said.

She looked at me, tears streaming down her cheeks. "How does he know all this?" It sounded like a plea rather than a question.

"Life is sacred," he said. "We must be careful what we dream." He touched her hands. His gentleness reminded me of my grandmother. His face broke into a toothless grin. "There are many ways to prevent pregnancy." This elicited a tentative smile from her.

He turned to me. His expression had once again become serious. "Your people," he said, "must learn to separate dreams from fantasies."

A long silence followed. Manco stared into his candle. Pauline looked down. Her fingers toyed with the end of her belt. Around us, the room was quiet. I knew that all eyes were glued to Manco. Every person there was wondering what he would do next.

His whistling began again. The little flame danced wildly. I thought he was too far away for his breath to be the cause of the candle's activity, but since there was no other breeze, I assumed that must be it. The flame leapt from side to side. Once it appeared to go out, then miraculously it revived. It took me back to my childhood, when I used to think I saw the spirits of Algonquian warriors dancing in our fireplace on a cold winter's night.

"Do you want to be cured?" His voice echoed through the stillness of that room.

She looked up.

"You must first make me a promise." He paused. "That you will return here in a couple of years." She started to respond, but he continued. "With your new husband and baby." A smile lighted his face.

She beamed. "You mean I can still have a child?"

"You will be able to."

When I finished translating, I could feel the tension leave the room. There was a general rustling, whispers, and the sound of people sighing their relief.

Manco stood abruptly. He moved remarkably fast for a man of his years. He retrieved a chair from a corner near the door and carried it into the circle, motioning for Pauline to sit on it. Then he indicated that she should remove her clothes.

The healing began immediately. Manco used a combination of techniques common to Quechua-speaking shamans. He executed each with great confidence and energy.

He sprayed a mist of trago through a burning candle into several branches of stinging nettles. While the branches were still engulfed in a halo of flames he shook them vigorously against Pauline's bare upper body. He repeated this on the area around her ovaries. He did this three times, all the while chanting in a low voice.

With great ceremony he gently massaged her with two of his sacred stones, one in each hand, careful to cover every inch of her, from head to toe. Next, he sprayed her with a light blanket of trago, followed by a fragrant oil.

He disappeared through the door. A few minutes later he returned. Stepping close to her, he blew. Out of his mouth, like a swarm of butterflies, flew carnation petals. They stuck to the oil and trago on her skin. She had a distant, tranquil look in her eyes.

He selected a couple of eggs from among the items displayed along his tapestry. On his knees, holding the eggs before her face, he sang a long song in Quechua. Then he placed an egg against her ovary and sucked violently on it. He quickly broke the egg into a clay pot and repeated the process with the other egg.

Finally he rose. He held the pot up as if offering it to the sky and took it outside.

When he came back, he shook a large, fanlike leaf over her head and down each side of her body. Chanting softly, he continued this for several minutes. At the end of each pass, he swished the leaf vigorously away from her as if driving something out of her body.

After he had finished, he stood behind her and, cupping his hands into a funnel, blew into the top of her head. Standing back, he looked at me and said that he would prescribe some herbs we could buy the next morning in the local market. Then he took her hands in his and helped her up.

Photo by John Perkins

FIGURE 10   Otavalan woman in traditional dress

The entire ceremony had taken perhaps forty-five minutes. Manco had expended a great deal of energy in the process. For Pauline it might have been an exhausting, even traumatic, experience. Yet both looked refreshed.

Pauline thanked him profusely, then turned to me. Her face was radiant. Someone came up and helped her into her clothes. She threw her arms around me. "How can I ever thank you?" she said. She walked back to the others. They hovered about her, offering sweaters and hugs and asking questions. I overheard her assuring them that the nettles had not hurt.

I went to Manco. Our hands met. "There are others here who need a cleansing," he said. "Afterward I would like to see you alone."

Manco healed two more people that evening. One was a medical doctor from Chicago who suffered from chronic neck pain. The other had struggled for years with two herniated disks in her lower back. He diagnosed them both without being told a thing by any of us; then he employed techniques similar to those he had used on Pauline. Both people felt immediate relief. That was evident to the rest of us not only through their testimonials but also from their appearances. Like Pauline, their eyes had a sparkle; they seemed, as someone put it, to glow.

Manco apparently gained energy as he proceeded. He never faltered or showed any sign of tiredness or lack of concentration. On the contrary, his chanting became more robust, his body more animated. The only break occurred when he summoned a granddaughter to cut additional nettles. She entered the room with her baby strapped to her back, then introduced herself to each of us, passing elegantly around the circle in her long blue wool skirt and embroidered white blouse, the traditional outfit of Otavalan women. Her baby peered at us with large brown eyes. Once or twice I thought I caught the suggestion of a smile, but he never made a sound.

I was in a state of constant excitement the whole time, which must have lasted nearly two and a half hours. Although I had witnessed similar healings, there was something special about these. I could not clear my mind of the sense of familiarity I felt for Manco or of the fact that he had asked me to meet with him later. My thoughts often wandered while I sat there watching him work, wondering why he had singled me out and what he would say or do to me.

As the others filed slowly from the room after the last of the healings, I lingered behind. A bit self-conscious, I wandered over to the tapestry and pretended to examine the sacred items. I found myself drawn to the hatchet head. I picked it up. It warmed to my touch. I stared directly at it and felt that I was being carried into it. It was as if the dark stone were absorbing me. Then a hand touched my shoulder.

"Very ancient," Manco said. "Powerful." He lifted my hand and placed it next to my heart. I could feel the huaca throbbing there, as though it were a living organ.

He took one of the candles and led me to a corner. The flame illuminated a small wooden trunk on the floor. Handing me the candle, he opened it and took something out. He kneeled in front of the trunk. I did likewise. He thrust his fist beneath the candle and slowly uncurled his fingers. What I saw took my breath away.

There in the palm of his wrinkled hand lay a tiny leather pouch I recognized, although I could not quite place where I had seen it before. I was transfixed by it, unbelieving and yet at the same time filled with curiosity. Then those earlier dreams flashed before me. I stared at it, amazed by the realization that it had been part of my life for a long time. At last I forced my eyes away from it. They met his.

"Have you ever heard of the Birdmen?" he asked.

His eyes dropped to the pouch. He watched it carefully as I described the Birdman ceremony I had attended so many years before, during my Peace Corps days: the beating of the drums, the melancholic music of Andean flutes, the way the dancing circle of Quechuas, cloaked in feathers and flapping gigantic condor wings, had entered into altered states and flown off to receive messages for the community from ancient beings.*

He showed no surprise that I had witnessed this ceremony, which few non-Quechua ever hear about, much less attend.

"Part of the job of the Birdmen," he said, "is to remold the human community."

"I don't understand."

He gave me a peculiar little grin as if we shared a secret. "No games," was all he said. And I realized with a shock that I did understand the meaning of his statement. He reached into the trunk once again and retrieved a small bottle, no longer than my thumb and about twice as thick.

We stood together and walked toward his huacas. I was vaguely aware of the hushed voices of my friends as we passed the open doorway. Through it I could see only stars in a black sky, no sign of any people. We sat side by side at the edge of his tapestry. I set the candle down in the spot where it had been during the earlier healings.

"All communities need remolding from time to time," he said. "It happened here when the Incas conquered us." He pulled the cork from the top of the bottle. "And again when the Spanish came." He set the cork and bottle down beside the candle. "Now is a time for remolding your commu-

---

*This ceremony is described in John Perkins, *Psychonavigation: Techniques for Travel beyond Time* (Rochester, Vt.: Destiny Books, 1990), chapter 4.

nity." Holding the leather pouch before the flame, he began to chant. It was the softest chanting I had ever heard, just barely audible. I kept expecting it to grow louder. Instead it stopped.

He rubbed the pouch between his hands. Then he gave it to me, indicating that I too should rub it. When I had finished, he opened it and turned it upside down over his palm. Yellow nuggets poured out. They sparkled in the candlelight like Incan gold.

He lifted his hand, and I saw that they were kernels of corn. He cupped his palm and, tipping it above the bottle, watched intently as they rolled inside. Again he chanted in the lowest voice imaginable.

As I searched my memory to try to bring back a recollection that seemed to hover in the mists of my subconscious, he took a swig of trago. He extended the hand that held the tiny bottle and with the other picked up the candle and positioned it between his mouth and the bottle.

He blew the trago through the flaming candle so suddenly that the explosive sound echoed through the room. The bottle was enveloped in a ball of flame.

"The seed is the dream of what is to be," he said, then resumed the low chanting.

As the flame died, I studied his hand, fearful that it had been scorched. But there was no sign of burned flesh. Inside the bottle, the kernels floated in a sea of liquid where the last remaining glow slowly faded. Manco placed the cork back inside the neck and pushed it firmly down.

"Remolding requires only that we change our dream. For this we must plant new seeds." He laid the bottle between my hands and pressed against them with his own. Now his chanting grew louder, but it did not approach the levels it had reached during the healings.

"My teacher, Sinchi, gave me those seeds," he said as we walked to the door. "Now they are yours, and I will be your teacher." He turned me to face him and hugged me briefly.

We stood in the open space just outside his room and looked up into the night together. "Come to me to help your people." His voice was like the chant. "You do not have to be in these mountains to consult with me. Come any time."

9

Learning from Manco

In my early thirties, I had gone through a very emotional divorce. I had sought help from a psychologist who, over a period of several years, helped me change how I viewed and approached my life. Ever since, during times of emotional crisis, I have heard Dr. Bernie's soothing voice coaxing me to explore my true feelings and to deal with them honestly.

I know that I am not unique in this. I have talked with many people, from all walks of life, who have experienced similarly powerful presences; often it is a parent or teacher whose voice they hear when they need advice. There is nothing mystical or religious about such experiences. We are simply responding to memories the way we were trained since infancy. When our parents punished us, for example, they would say things like, "Next time you even think about doing that, remember what I'm telling you now!" Rewards for good behavior are calculated to accomplish the same effect. Recollections of praise are one of the strongest motivators in our early— and perhaps later—lives.

In the case of Manco, it is more than a voice. His presence is total. I feel him, see him, even smell him. I journey to sit next to him between Grandmother Cotacachi and Grandfather Imbabura.

Sometimes Manco attends my workshops in the United States. Although he teaches many techniques for helping us become more fulfilled personally, more centered and present in the moment, his objective is always the same: to teach us to recognize our unity with all else, and in doing this remold ourselves so that we move forward into a new dream.

"To *camay*," Manco explained, "is to breathe unity into. No corresponding word exists in Spanish. Even the idea is difficult to express, for it seems that you northerners don't believe such things. In our lives, it is a very important concept, perhaps the most important. We have several related words: *churay, ruray,* and *supay*. These have to do with creating. But *camay* is the most powerful."

He knelt before a gnarled old agave, a special plant to Andean people

96

that is related to the aloe. "This plant appeared to be dead a year ago. I camayed into it every day, and now look." He patted it tenderly. "Old, but very much alive." He stood. "We are all one." He turned slowly in a circle, his hands at his sides, palms out. "When one of our parts is out of balance, others can help bring them back. That is when we camay."

A little boy approached us. Without hesitation, he grabbed the edge of Manco's poncho and held it. Manco spoke softly to him in Quechua, then reached down and took the boy's hand in his own. We walked on. "The blowing we do during a healing is a form of camaying. We breathe unity into the sick or injured person to restore balance."

"Sort of an infusing of spirit," I observed.

"Yes," Manco replied, but his voice seemed to question. The path took a bend to the right around a small hill. "*Spirit* is a complex word. Its meaning changes depending on the language you speak. For the Spanish I think it does not reflect the unity of all things as it does for us."

I was tempted to argue that the Holy Spirit was, indeed, a universal spirit, but I realized that the way it is usually presented diminishes its powers, or at least relegates them to a rather impersonal level. "Did Christ camay?"

He never broke his stride. "I have spent many hours in the Catholic church. It is a difficult religion. The priests are very confused about their beliefs. They talk about them all the time, yet have difficulty using them. Yes, from all I've heard, Christ was a great shaman. He healed people, animals, and plants. He healed rocks, rivers, minerals, and the sky. He camayed."

As we completed the turn around the hill, a spectacular vista of Cotacachi opened before us. I stopped. "Manco, can you camay Grandmother Cotacachi?"

"She is far more balanced than me. She camays me." He laughed. We sat down. The little boy climbed up onto his knee.

I pressed him further, asking how far a person could take the camaying process.

"There are no limits. We are all one, everything you see around you and way beyond. All the stars in the night sky and the invisible ones. If a part of this wonderful dream is out of balance, we dream it right. We camay it."

"So you could camay Grandmother Cotacachi?"

"If she were out of balance, but she is not."

"And Pachamama?"

"If she were out of balance." He looked at me. "But she is not. We humans are the ones who need to be camayed."

"Can you camay a whole species?"

There was a long pause. I could hear the boy humming a soft melody

Photo by Ehud C. Sperling

FIGURE 11   Cotopaxi, the world's highest active volcano

and realized that he had not understood a word of our Spanish conversation. I reached over and patted his head. His eyes smiled into mine, but only briefly. "It can be done," Manco said. "It must be done. That is why we are here together."

It seemed the appropriate time to bring up the thing that was haunting me. Only recently had I understood the sense of familiarity I felt toward this man. "I dreamed about you many years ago."

"Of course," he said. "That is how it happens."

"But this was different." I told him about the dreams I had had while a student at Middlebury College of the young boy who became a quipu camayoc runner and the later dreams about the old shaman living high in the Andes.

"I had those same dreams," he said. "And they came true." He gave the boy on his lap a squeeze. "With both of us dreaming them, how could they not have?"

"But," I protested, "those were nighttime dreams; they happened while I was actually sleeping."

He merely nodded.

I thought about this and realized that I still had a great deal to learn. Then a question entered my mind. Before I could ask, he said, "Have you thought about the word *camayoc*?"

It floored me, for he had read my mind. The relationship of that word to *camay* had been my question.

"*Quipu camayoc.*" He smiled gently. "What does it mean?"

"They were the relay runners who tied the Incan Empire together by carrying messages quickly from one end to the other."

"Not exactly." He took a deep breath and let it out slowly. "Strictly speaking, they were the interpreters of the messages. The messages, called quipus, were in the form of colored strings of yarn knotted into special codes that were difficult to read. These were carried by runners between the quipu camayocs, those who had been trained to 'breathe wholeness' into the quipus, making it possible to understand the messages. So you see, a quipu camayoc was a sort of cultural shaman, a very powerful person indeed, for the future of the kingdom might rest in his ability to camay a ball of intricately knotted string. In order to reach this status, he had to complete many years of training. Once he made it to that exalted position, he quite literally held the secrets of the empire within his fingers." The boy slipped down from his lap and took off after a butterfly. "I think our species needs some good quipu camayocs now," Manco said. "To unravel the complex web of knots we have tied ourselves up in."

"Fantasies," Manco said, laughing, "are wonderful. We all have them, and that is good, but we mustn't confuse them with dreams. When I was a young man I lusted after my neighbor's wife, a woman I had known as a dear friend all my life. Now that she was married and living in the house next door, I wanted to make love with her. I fantasized all the time about this. Incredible fantasies! So incredible that it became my dream. And of course it happened. Dreams always do. It was delightful too. But afterward—oh, what trouble it caused me! You see, it really shouldn't have been a dream, just a beautiful fantasy. My confusion hurt a lot of people; it destroyed the friendship she and I had previously shared."

"How do you distinguish between fantasies and dreams?"

He gave me that grin I had become accustomed to. "You know the difference. We all do—deep in here." He patted his chest. "Fantasies can affect us strongly, but we don't want them to come true—we just want to experience them vicariously. Dreams work to change our lives. We convince ourselves that we can't discriminate, all the while knowing perfectly well that we can. Did I really want to make love with that woman? Yes, but not just that. What I wanted was to live with her, to marry her. My problem was I didn't give that dream the energy it deserved. Once she married another, I should have been content with the fantasies and recognized them for what they were. You see, because we are all branches of the same tree, we vibrate to each other's dreams. By giving our dreams energy we empower them to happen, and the next thing we know—poof, there we are."

"In bed with our neighbor's wife."

"In the cornfield with my dear friend. Yes, exactly. That or whatever. So, John, it is very important that people learn to separate fantasies from dreams." He turned and headed down the path toward Mount Imbabura.

"Your people," he continued, "have great difficulty distinguishing between the two. You are overly rational, depend too much on the modern fantasy that science can answer all the questions and turn the world into a giant playground for rich gringos. You have convinced yourselves that you can control Pachamama, a fantasy that is wonderfully entertaining, but one that as a dream is terribly destructive."

"Like the one about your friend, your neighbor's wife."

"Exactly. It hurts people, on a huge scale. And a lot of other things also: plants, animals, rocks, the sky and rivers. A tremendous amount of energy is generated by your people. Since you set an example for so much of the rest of the world, this is magnified over and over. So it is important that your people stop turning fantasies into dreams." We sat on a grassy knoll.

I told him that I had been in touch with some of the people he had healed and that they were doing well. "The woman with the herniated disk has not suffered any pain since she was here. The doctor's neck is completely better."

"And the woman who lost her baby?"

"A week after you healed her, her gynecologist found that the tumor was gone. She is feeling very well and looking forward to seeing you again." We watched a bird land on a small bush. "Your healing has helped a lot of people."

"I don't heal," he corrected. "I simply help them change their dream."

"You mean to tell me they could do it just as well without you?"

"Sometimes we need the permission of another," he said, without taking his eyes off the bird. "Sometimes we need a guide. We need to feel the spirits around us to help us understand that we are all one. A person trained in such things can find a clear path, one that cuts straight through all the fallen trees."

"A shaman."

"Everyone has the power to be a shaman." He anticipated my question. "The first step is to learn to separate dreams from fantasies. That woman gave too much energy to her fantasy. She became pregnant with a baby she didn't want. In order to realize her new dream—of not being a mother—her body developed an energy that later threatened her life. The guilt and sadness she felt kept her locked into a dream that was destructive."

"Until you came along."

"I simply helped her bring things into balance. I offered another dream. She has done the rest."

Recalling the many books I had read on shamanism, I asked him what role spirits play. He seemed surprised by the question, responding that of course spirits are everywhere. Then he returned to the old theme I had heard so many times from him, the Shuar, and other traditional elders. "We are all the same, branches of one tree that springs from a single seed," he said. "You and I, the spirits, Pachamama herself. The power of the dream is the power of our unity."

"What happens when we destroy parts of Pachamama?"

"We break the circle, diminishing the power. But the circle heals quickly, unless there are too many breaks and they are large. When you cut a tree here or there, Pachamama bleeds a little. Then, like a person pricked with a thorn, she heals. But when you bulldoze forests, the healing takes a long time. These days, there is massive bleeding. One wound upon another. Pachamama suffers terribly."

I remembered Numi's comment and, interested in Manco's reaction, asked whether he thought Pachamama herself was in danger or whether she would simply treat us like troublesome fleas and shake us off.

"We and Pachamama are the same. We suffer terribly along with her. People everywhere are bleeding. The seeds I gave you? Yes, in the bottle. You must plant them. A new dream will sprout to spread its powerful branches."

This did not satisfy my curiosity. "But is it possible that we will not survive and Pachamama will?"

"We are all one." He watched me closely. "Be careful, my friend, not to become too engrossed in reason. Remember, the idea that science can answer all the questions is a fantasy. When you ask that question I think you have science in mind. Ask yourself what survival means. What were we before we were humans?"

"I have no idea."

"Exactly. But we were part of this whole. Our dream, Pachamama's dream, resulted in this." He ran his hands slowly down his body, a gesture that was reminiscent of the way he diagnosed illness. "If the dream becomes too painful, it will change. But survival—what does it mean?"

He stood and headed back up the path. I knew the session was coming to a close. I caught up with him. "How do we help this process, change the dream?"

"The Birdmen. The community must remold itself. Start with the seeds."

I grabbed the edge of his poncho. "Please, Manco," I pleaded. "Some practical advice."

"You want me to outline the basic steps for dream change?" He threw his head back and laughed. I felt disheartened. When he turned to look me in the eye, his expression was serious. I knew what he would say; he was going to tell me that I already knew the steps.

"Later," he said instead, his eyes twinkling.

It was early morning. We were walking down by the lake where the women and young girls washed their families' clothes. They wore the traditional white blouses embroidered with brightly colored designs, their long skirts tucked up so they could wade in the shallow water. The Otavalan people are exceptionally attractive, and in this setting, with the sun barely peeking over the horizon and a low mist clinging to the reeds along the shore, the women looked as though they had just emerged from an artist's dream.

"Education," Manco told me, "is the key. The way a people educate its children determines how they will distinguish fantasies from dreams. This is true for the whole culture as well as individuals." He paused long enough to chat briefly with several women.

"You people have brought your education to us," he continued. "In our schools, the children get the benefit of models developed by the Spanish, French, Italians, Germans, and North Americans. They see photos taken from outer space, come home to tell their parents about doctors who transplant hearts and kidneys. They learn your alphabet. They become proficient at reading, writing, and calculating numbers. They understand that a chemical factory on the other side of Pachamama killed hundreds of people and that a power plant blew radiation everywhere. But..." He paused, looking about. "The schools don't teach them that." He pointed at a mother who was showing her daughter how to wade through the reeds without breaking them. "Your education system has brought us soap; it has not taught us how to keep the soap from destroying our water. Fortunately, we still remember the reeds. Our elders teach us that Pachamama has ways of taking care of herself, as long as we don't overburden her, as long as we cherish and help her. I wonder, though, how long we will continue to remember. The schools do not give prizes for knowledge like that."

I thought about the society created by the educational system that had evolved in the so-called civilized world, trying to recall statistics about crime, poverty, and ecological destruction. "I recently read," I said to him, "that children in the United States consume more than thirty times the amount of resources consumed by children in countries like Ecuador."

He stopped, cocked his head to one side, and gave me a quizzical look. "We live very well here." He spread his arms to the countryside. "Sometimes I lament that we have too much. Every generation grows a little taller. That is not good. Soon we will all look like gringos." He chuckled. "We should not take as much as we do from Pachamama. What do your children do with all those things?"

"They become terribly spoiled." It was the only answer I could think of.

We moved on, leaving the women at the lake behind. The great volcano Imbabura loomed in front of us. Mists circled its summit. During the next few minutes I picked my way carefully over the uneven path, my eyes glued to it as we walked. When I looked up, I was shocked to see that Imbabura had disappeared, replaced by a white cloud.

"Prosperity," Manco told me, "is having enough of what we need when we need it." He picked up a stick and drew two circles in the sand, one about a quarter the size of the other. "Your people," he said, pointing at the larger, see this very differently from mine." The stick moved to the smaller circle. "For us prosperity is clean air and water, living close to Pachamama and our families, and eating fresh foods that we or our neighbors have grown with loving care. It is the knowledge, learned from daily living, that we all are one. It is honoring and protecting our mother, knowing that our grandfather is always here for us."

He raised the stick and pointed at Imbabura. I was amazed to see that the cloud had dissolved. The massive volcano stood there before us in all its majesty. For a moment I wondered whether my eyes had been playing tricks. I felt like I was in a land of dreams and that the distinction between reality and magic had vanished.

"Parallel worlds," Manco said, as though he had read my thoughts.

We walked farther on in silence. I could tell that the discussion had affected him deeply. He muttered something. When I asked him what he had said, he told me only that it had been the Quechua word for *birth*. Then he turned to me. "You need a new type of education."

"We do," I agreed.

"One of my sons is a teacher," he said. "He and I often talk about how important it is for children to understand the oneness of all things. Yet he tells me the schools insist on teaching about separateness. Everything is broken down into meaningless categories and studied at the smallest level possible. Why?"

"Science believes," I responded, "that if you understand all the parts of a thing, you understand the thing itself."

"And the other things that this thing is part of?"

"It has not been an important question for science. At least not until recently. Hopefully, the old approach is changing."

"It must change. And my son also tells me that the schools do not want children to talk with Pachamama, Inti, and Mama Kilya, with the birds, plants, and rocks, or with any of the guiding spirits and animals."

"Conversations with these spirits and guides are not consistent with the approach we have put so much faith in. Ours is a hard, 'rational' approach that sees humans perched at the top of a pedestal."

We continued walking. After a pause, Manco said, "Education for us

includes traveling into the parallel worlds, to the past and future, in order
to understand and change our dreams." I thought about the encouragement given to small children throughout the Andes to venture into what
we in my culture refer to as altered states of consciousness. "The past and
future," he continued, "are dreams of those worlds." We had arrived at a
shallow stream, and he stopped and poked at a stone with his stick.
"Through dream change we are able to change the past and future. He
turned to face me. "Of course, this also alters the present."

We crossed the stream by stepping from stone to stone. As we walked
on toward Imbabura, I thought of the many times I had worried about a
future event, only to discover that it was not nearly as threatening as I had
expected. I realized that fear is often nothing more than the anticipation of
pain. It is a dream—a nightmare—that is probably based on some association with a memory of another event in the past—another dream—that
somehow appears to be connected to the one we expect in the future. Indeed, by changing the dream, either the one in the past or the one in the
future, we can alleviate—or amplify—the fear.

"The energy created by our dreaming," Manco continued, "is like the
air. It travels everywhere." He stopped and peered into my eyes as if his
were journeying into my very soul. "Your ability to use this energy is lim-
ited only by your dream of its power." He paused a long moment. "Your
faith." His eyes were like magnets, pulling mine to them.

"Our dreams can affect everyone and everything else—if we energize
them with enough power." He gave me a searching look. "Do you believe
this, John?"

I thought for a moment. I had come to trust him completely and to
believe in the shamanic healings and psychonavigational abilities I had seen
and experienced time and again. But I did not want my answer to sound
casual; I wanted to frame it in the context of my own culture. "Yes," I said
at last, "I absolutely do. You know, we in the United States say that a person must be careful of the friends he keeps, because one person's energy
'rubs off' onto another. If you hang around with negative people, with 'los-
ers,' you become negative yourself." Manco was observing me carefully.
"On the other hand, a confident leader instills confidence in everyone around
him. Even before I began studying with you, I knew this. What you have
taught me reinforces it."

He smiled. "So the ways we are taught to dream are not all that different after all."

I had to think about that. "Well, actually, they are extremely different,
like night and day." Then it struck me. "But deep down, of course, we are
all one. So we are not different at all." We both laughed.

While we walked, I continued to turn this over in my mind. "If we are one," I asked him as we arrived at the top of a knoll that gave us a spectacular view of the entire valley, "then why do my people look at the world so differently from yours?"

"In the time of the ancestors," Manco told me, "the people of the Andes became obsessed with greed. Inti had sent his sweat to Pachamama in the form of gold. Mama Kilya had sent her teardrops as silver. These were threads to weave the dreams of those three great spirits—Sun, Moon, and Earth—together. They were sacred, and the people were to use them only in sacred ways, for dreaming, worship, meditation, and spiritual journeying. But the people forgot their duties and began to collect the gold and silver selfishly. They thought of them as wealth, 'prosperity,' and hoarded them. Then Viracocha, the Great Creator, grew angry at these foolish people, my ancestors. He ordered his son, Eagle, to fly out of the heavens and down to Pachamama to visit the people of the Andes and teach them a new dream. Ever since that time, my people have practiced Eagle's teachings. We call this dream change. And we are Birdpeople."

Manco explained that dream change combines the knowledge he had outlined to me with the art of camaying. "Remember: the energy created through our dreaming ties us all together, and we have ultimate power," he said. "When we camay this power into ourselves and all that is around us—part of our very oneness—we can create anything we dream. But," he held up a single finger, "you must understand that when the dream is negative, or when we deceive ourselves into mistaking fantasies for dreams, the creation can be a monster of nightmarish proportions. That is what happened to the people of the Andes during the time of my ancestors. It is happening now, once again, this time to your people. Yes, yours look at the world very differently from mine. They have given energy to their fantasies. They have become deceived, believing that gold, silver, and other material goods will buy them happiness. But Eagle is even now wandering among your people. His power brought you here. You bring and teach others, and they teach still others. We are all one. Sometimes we look at things differently. Through dream change we will all become Birdpeople."

The first step of the dream-change process, he emphasized, is to define what we want, to make certain that it is a dream, not a fantasy. "Psychonavigation can be a big help in this regard, as can power animals and inner pilots. Make sure that it is a positive dream." He added that an essential next step is to give the dream energy. "Constantly bring your dream out into the light of day. Think about it, meditate and journey on it. Talk about it with everyone you meet. Shout it out. Share it with the Earth, the sky, the clouds, the sun and moon, and with all the plants, animals, and minerals of the Earth. Give it voice and song!"

"If people tell you it is a foolish or impossible dream," he continued, "immediately correct them. Reverse their negativity by insisting that it is a dream that must and will happen. Never allow anyone to take the energy out of your dream by weighing it down with negativity or doubt." He suggested citing examples of other "impossible" dreams that have come true, like the demise of communism in Eastern Europe. "What forty years and billions of CIA dollars couldn't accomplish was done overnight by a handful of poets!"

Manco emphasized the potency of parallel worlds. "See yourself in one of those other worlds, enter it with all your senses, a world after your dream has come true. Experience that world over and over—a hundred times a day. Feel it, see it, hear, taste, and smell it. Understand with every part of your existence the wonders and pleasures of your dream fulfilled."

He reminded me once again that dream-change energy is everywhere, like the air, tying everything together. "You must camay this energy all the time. And when you do this, you will see that your dream will be realized quicker than you ever expected." He laughed. "Just be careful. Remember always my neighbor's wife. Let her be your conscience. Let her protect you from fantasies." He paused and gave me a long, hard look. "Direct your energies, your incredible power, toward positive dreams, ones that bring true prosperity to you and Pachamama." Then his face broke into a wonderful grin. "As your friend Numi said, the world is as you dream it. I will only add that you must work on it."

10

Passing On the Dream

Taking groups of medical and other professionals to Ecuadoran shamans, as well as pursuing my work with Manco, had a strong impact on the workshops I held in the United States. Previously I had conducted them in a purely businesslike manner, avoiding anything that smacked of the exotic. After seeing the positive effects of drumming, music, incense, and other rituals on the people who accompanied me to Ecuador, however, I began to incorporate aspects of those practices into the workshops. The changes were received enthusiastically. I grew bolder, and eventually my sessions began to look, sound, and even smell like those held in a shaman's lodge. Manco was a skilled instructor whose teachings about ceremony, as well as healing and psychonavigation, brought many improvements to the work I was doing.

Many of the workshop participants reported amazing results from their own efforts at camaying. Examples included household plants that suddenly began to bloom after they had been camayed and sick animals who were brought back to health; several people described healing their own injuries—a broken toe, an infected insect bite, migraine headaches. Many were therapists who adapted the techniques to their own professions and used them to help patients with an array of emotional as well as physical problems.

Taking a hint from what Manco had said about the quipu camayocs' being cultural shamans and the need to camay a whole species, I hit upon the idea of bringing change to entire professions. During the workshops we camayed the medical doctors to focus on healing the balance between humankind and nature; the lawyers to see their primary job as protecting the rights of all plants, animals, and minerals; the teachers to teach long-term sustainability; the economists to preserve the economic viability of Earth; and the religious leaders to preserve the natural world as the primary revelation of the divine.

"We often refer to our 'sixth sense,'" I told the sixty people seated on mats in a circle at my workshop. "But I think this is really a reference to a whole group of nonphysical phenomena, including not only the dream senses

107

but also the creative, healing, and destructive powers of our perceptions. These are not recognized by modern Western science because they defy the scientists' abilities to measure and quantify. Yet we all know they are real."

It is a discussion I have had with myself often. I know, for example, that perception is the key to the way we live. Whether we choose to perceive an event as good or bad, as making us happy or sad, truly determines how that event will affect us. I have found time and again that altering my perception changes the world; it can be hostile and forbidding or warm and sheltering, depending on how I view it.

"Every martial artist," I continued, "will tell you that strength has nothing to do with breaking concrete blocks. Children can succeed where weight lifters fail. The only thing that matters is perception. If you perceive the block as a solid rock that will shatter your bones, you will fail. If you see it as a potato chip and visualize your hand slicing easily through it, you will succeed."

A woman in the circle raised her hand. "There are many stories," she said, "about how the American Indians were unable to see the ships of the early European explorers because such things were beyond their perception. I believe it was Captain Cook who wrote about how he had to take a chief and his warriors by canoe out to his ship and make them touch it before they could see it."

"Like UFOs today," someone volunteered. This brought chuckles from around the circle.

I told them about my attempts to lead people along Shuar trails through the jungle. I would always end up getting hopelessly lost, the trail apparently dissolving into the forest. Then a Shuar would step to the front and guide us directly to the trail; as soon as he did this, the vegetation would appear to open up before us. Even to me, the trail would be obvious, but only for as long as a Shuar was leading. "Somehow, in ways I can't explain, being in the presence of the guide's superior perception improves, at least temporarily, my own ability to perceive."

As I talk about these subjects at my workshops, I often see Manco's face and I feel as though he is helping me. It is not that I am acting as his channel; I do not feel that he somehow has taken possession of me and is speaking through me. Rather, he is like my coach, standing on the sidelines or in the prompter's box, guiding and encouraging me and sometimes feeding me a couple of lines in order to facilitate my explanations.

Participants take a strong interest in the healings I have witnessed and the shamanic belief that we all have the power to heal ourselves. We discuss ways our bodies fight infectious diseases and heal wounds. Often this leads to conversations about biofeedback, acupuncture, massage therapy, and other forms of mind-body healing that are gaining popularity among people raised in the Western scientific medical tradition.

The opposite of the healing sense is the destructive sense. It is generally accepted by shamans—and increasingly among many in our own population—that we have the power to bring illness and pain upon ourselves and others. Our reactions to stressful situations and to familial patterns such as alcoholism affect our health. Within each of us is a force—call it a "sense"—that determines the "feel" of any given situation, causing us to become depressed or exhilarated, active or passive. This force may be closely aligned with perception, and yet it appears to go beyond it, triggering chemical responses deep in our hormonal structure.

Our reactions, our moods, can affect others in powerful ways. When I was a boy growing up in rural New Hampshire, my parents were convinced that wet feet caused colds. If you stepped in a puddle, you had to change your shoes and socks immediately or you would get sick. And in fact, experience bore them out. I found that whenever I did not follow their advice in this regard, I would catch a cold—no exceptions. I also was continually frustrated to see that this rule did not apply to some of my schoolmates; I assumed that they were just heartier. Then, many years later, I discovered that I could spend days in the rain forests with wet feet. My Shuar companions assured me that no harm would come of this. And they too were correct! I have since found that I now can get wet feet in New Hampshire without contracting a cold.

"The shamans," I continued, "use this other group of senses to travel into the parallel worlds. Once there, they rely on the five physical senses to help them understand and interpret what they find." I turned to Sally, a psychotherapist who had recently returned from one of my trips to Ecuador, and asked her to share her impressions.

"For me, the information these men and woman brought back from their psychonavigational journeys was amazing," she said. "They learned things about me and the others that absolutely boggled our minds. And yes, their experiences once in these other worlds were highly sensual. Like John says, they seemed to have a whole set of 'other' senses that got them there. But then, they used the traditional ones—sight, touch, smell, taste, and hearing—to access knowledge and to heal us." She sighed. "What can I say? They are incredibly powerful."

People shifted in the circle to get a better view of Sally. They asked questions and encouraged her to describe her personal experiences. At one point the conversation shifted to ayahuasca.

Sally glanced around the circle of faces and smiled self-consciously. "Ayahuasca forces us to change our perceptions, to leave our bodily consciousness, to see the world differently. It is life-changing, but so is the shamanic work done without it. I think dream change is what is needed in this unbalanced world where we've become so preoccupied with the material sides of life. Whether we use ayahuasca or some other tool to change our dream really isn't important. The important thing is that we make the change."

The room was silent. I turned on a tape I had recorded of Kitiar playing his tumank. We all sat quietly listening. Sally had spoken eloquently, and the power of her words seemed to fill the room. I saw Manco where he sat meditating between Grandmother Cotacachi and Grandfather Imbabura. It occurred to me that the shamans were reemerging. It seemed as though they had gone into hiding during the Spanish Inquisition and remained there for the ensuing invasions by missionaries, capitalists, and medical doctors who refused to recognize their powers. Now, precisely when the imbalance between humans and Pachamama threatened to destroy us as a species, the shamans were coming forward once again to help us reconnect with nature, to help us feel our unity, our oneness, with the plant, mineral, and animal worlds. Sally had experienced the shaman's power firsthand, and now she was carrying their message to the sixty people seated in a circle. Her story, along with their recent psychonavigations, was even now changing those people.

I stood up and walked among them, beating my drum softly. As I wandered about the seated participants, I realized that the shamans had not really gone into hiding at all. They had continued to practice, but only among their own people, and quietly. Unlike the missionaries, they had never attempted to convert others. Perhaps they had known that their energies would be needed. Perhaps they had been conserving their powers for this moment of crisis. If we truly live in parallel worlds, if everything is one, and it is all occurring concurrently, then all the shamans are here now, ready to help us. Their power is awesome. This would explain why so many people—including traditional medical doctors and psychologists—are suddenly being drawn to them.

I let the drumbeat taper off and returned to my place in the circle. Kitiar's piece ended. I turned off the tape. "Any questions for Sally, comments, or thoughts?"

The people stirred. I could see that in their own ways they too had been journeying. They were returning to the world of the room, the workshop, and the circle. Someone asked her to be more specific about the life-changing aspect.

She smiled sweetly and shrugged. "Oh, so many things happened that altered my view of my life." She hesitated, glanced down at her hands where they lay in her lap, and continued. "This may sound strange, but while I was psychonavigating I revisited times in my past." She gave me a look. "I suppose I went to one of those parallel worlds you like to talk about, John. I found that I could change my past, could alter the outcomes of events that happened to me long ago. And you know what? This has changed my attitude toward a lot of things and people." When pressed, she said that her relationship with her parents had improved immensely. Then a perplexed look crossed her face. She fidgeted. Apologetically, she explained that the experience was still too personal and too close for her to share it in detail.

Sensing her discomfort, I spoke up. "The past," I said, "is our dream of a memory. It is not a fact." I paused to allow this to sink in. "A perception. Everything we remember is filtered, like a dream being interpreted. Change the dream, change the memory, and you change the past." I recalled a healing I had done with a woman who had a terribly debilitating fear of heights. "When you change the past, you also alter the present and your dream of the future. This can be extremely powerful."

I told them the story of a woman who was afraid to cross bridges.

Although Josephine had a master's degree in psychology, she made a living as a public relations consultant operating out of Portland, Oregon. In college, she had developed a deep interest in shamanism. Her voice, at the other end of the telephone line, sounded agitated.

"I desperately want to take your trip to Ecuador," she said. "But if I do, will I have to cross that bridge?"

"The one pictured in my brochure?"

"Yeah. The swinging one. Like the bridge in an Indiana Jones movie."

I told her she would have to cross it if she intended to hike through the jungle to either the sacred falls or the thermal falls. She had stimulated

Figure 12   Shuar bridge

Photo by John Perkins

my curiosity, and it did not seem necessary to explain that if the river were low she might be able to wade across; otherwise, she could be ferried by canoe. From a shamanic point of view, it was important to hear her out and discover where the agitation originated. "Is there a problem?" I asked.

"Absolutely. A very serious one." She explained that since childhood she had been terrified of heights. In recent years, her phobia had grown worse. "Now," she added with a sigh, "I can't even cross a stream by stepping from rock to rock. It's that bad!"

This was indeed serious. I realized that she probably would not even be able to descend the steep slope down to the river, much less wade across it. And there were other questions. How could she scale the cliffs on the way to the thermal falls, or climb down into the volcano crater where Raul and I had planned to take the group to camp for one night? Would she be able to handle the flight into the jungle in the small plane that skimmed across the top of the canopy?

By coincidence—although I have come to believe that few things occur by coincidence alone—it so happened that I had recently scheduled a workshop in Seattle. When I related this to Josephine she was enthusiastic. "I'll be there for sure," she said. I explained that I would be staying at the home of some friends and suggested that maybe she could also spend the night following the workshop with them so that we might have a couple of hours together either that evening or early the next morning to work on her acrophobia problem.

"Are you telling me you can cure me?" she asked, the incredulity transmitted clearly from coast to coast across the telephone line.

"Psychonavigation can work miracles." I laughed. "Sometimes. We'll just have to wait and see about this one." I asked whether she had any ideas about what caused her fear of heights or when it had begun.

As for the cause, she could tell me nothing. She had been plagued by it ever since she could remember. "But," she added, "only recently has it been so severe, so completely debilitating. Before, I used to feel mildly apprehensive, sometimes a little dizzy and weak-kneed, but not like now. For over a year now, since I turned thirty-five, it has kept me from doing many things. And that never happened before."

The workshop in Seattle was a powerful one. Many of the attendees were well prepared. Most had read *Psychonavigation,* and many had also read *The Stress-Free Habit*. Since they already knew a great deal about me and the subject, I could dispense with most of the stories and explanations and move directly into the experiential work. I had them pair off to purify each other using the four elements; then each participant retrieved a power animal for his or her partner. We burned incense that is specially prepared for me by shamans, and accompanied by drums, rattles, and whistles, we danced and chanted. Then we moved into what I believe is the essence of shamanism: healing. Using techniques similar to those practiced by Andean shamans, I worked on three people, each with a different illness. Following that, as a group we completed a number of healings. Finally, we all camayed balance into the relationship between our culture and nature.

We closed with a brief discussion about how healing is a concrete example of the shaman's ability to use psychonavigational journeying to effect change. I reminded them that the world truly is as we dream it and emphasized once again that we all have the power to redream the world and to redefine the role humans play in it. As I looked around at their faces I felt confident that a majority of them intended to take my words to heart. They glowed, much the way people glow after being healed by an Otavalan, Salasacan, Cañari, Shuar, or Lowland Quichua shaman.

Josephine helped me pack up the huacas and other tools I use during workshops. Feeling her energy next to me, I had no doubt that soon her acrophobia would be gone, or a least greatly diminished.

We met in front of the living room fireplace at five-thirty the following morning. We would have two hours before joining our hosts for breakfast (I was scheduled to leave for the airport at nine). Outside, the rain in the trees reminded me of the rain forests. I mentioned this to Josephine, and together we stood at the window looking out into the darkness. "I want so badly to go," she sighed.

I lit a small fire along with a button of copal incense. We sat quietly facing each other for a few moments, the crackle of the fire blending with the patter of the rain. She began telling me about her fear, how it had grown from something that was merely an irritant to a disease that was—as she described it—robbing her of her life.

As we talked, I studied her carefully. I tried to perceive imbalances in her energy the way Manco had taught me to. After a while I began to notice a small dark area over the top of her head. When I asked her about it, she gave me an odd sort of look. Then, without further hesitation, she explained that it was due to something that had happened while she was in the womb. "My mother tried to abort me," she said unemotionally. "In the process, she injured my head."

"You're certain of this?"

"Yes, but how did you know?"

I explained that I could detect energy concentrated in that area and briefly described ways the "other" senses can be used to "see" such things. All the while I had a feeling that perhaps something other than an attempted abortion had been involved. I went to the fire and held my drum over it. I asked her whether she had ever heard of soul retrieval.

She had read Mircea Eliade's classic book *Shamanism: Archaic Techniques of Ecstasy*. We talked about the soul retrievals discussed by Eliade, whose primary focus had been on Central and North Asian tribes: the Tungus, Manchu, Tartars, Buryat, and others from similar traditions. She came to kneel beside me at the fire. "I have heard," she said with a slight tremor, "that soul retrieval is dangerous."

Several weeks earlier I had helped a man who had called me after a soul retrieval had been performed on him in New York City. I used his story as an example of how the process can go bad. "According to the Cuna Indians, who live on the San Blas Islands, off the coast of Panama, a part of the soul flies away whenever a person experiences a serious trauma," I said and described some of my personal experiences with the Cuna in the 1970s. "A good shaman is careful not to retrieve that part of the soul until his patient has dealt with the trauma that caused it to leave." Removing the drum from the fire, I handed it to her. She caressed it gently with her fingers. "Unfortunately, this New York man's therapist did not know—or at least did not honor—that tradition. He brought back the missing soul without first dealing with the trauma." She returned the drum. I began beating it softly and explained that such practices are fairly widespread. "They can be very painful for the patient. They have given the whole idea of soul retrieval a bad name. And to the extent that people are practicing this ancient technique without taking proper precautions, that bad name may be justified."

"Do I need a soul retrieval?"

I told her that I did not know the answer to her question, but since it was a possibility, had wanted her to understand the process. I assured her that I would not perform a soul retrieval unless I was certain we had first dealt with the cause of the trauma.

"You and I," I added, "are about to journey together to a special place, the place where your acrophobia originates. We will take the shortest and safest route possible. Aside from that, I can't tell you much."

Josephine lay down on her back next to the fireplace. The room was filled with the smell of copal combined with that of burning wood. The soft beat of the drum mingled with the sound of the rain outside. I told her that I would be using two of my power animals, a white female wolf and a female dolphin. I asked whether she was comfortable with the pony that had been retrieved for her at the workshop. Her facial expression as well as her words assured me that the pony would be a powerful presence. I reminded her that power animals help us "die," assisting in the transition out of our everyday world of materialism to other levels of consciousness. I explained that we would travel to wherever they took us, but that we should keep in mind her need to rid herself of her fear of heights.

The drum grew louder. I instructed her to call on her pony. The wolf and dolphin joined us immediately. The beat of the drum quickened. It was the sound of the pony's galloping hooves. She and I rode the pony. Wolf raced along beside us while dolphin swam through the air. We charged down a tunnel formed by lush trees with overhanging branches. It smelled of flowers. At the end we could see a light. We headed for it and soon found ourselves flying through a forest clearing, the wind whistling in our hair.

Suddenly the pony came to an abrupt stop, nearly throwing the two of us over his head. The wolf and dolphin stood beside us. Ahead was the bridge. I looked at Josephine and saw a mask of terror.

Dismounting, I assured her that everything would be all right. I offered her my hand. Although she took it and climbed down, I could feel her fear. She wanted to flee. I coaxed her on. Despite her reluctance, she acquiesced. Together we walked slowly along the trail to the bridge. She complained of the hot sun beating down on her shoulders, suggesting that we take cover under the shade of the trees. I told her there would be time to relax later. She tried to hold back, but I held firmly to her hand and took her to the step leading up to the bridge. She peered down its length. Her breaths came as gasps.

We stood there looking at the scene before us. Sunshine poured down through the clear space above the river, illuminating the bridge as though it were an actor caught in the spotlight on a gigantic stage. The drum grew louder. I told her I would be with her the whole time and assured her that no harm would come to her. Slowly—ever so very slowly—we inched our way out onto the bridge.

Although her fear was palpable, Josephine was extremely courageous. She kept moving forward. Step by step we proceeded. We moved away from the riverbank and out over the swirling rapids a hundred feet below. We reached a point approximately a quarter of the way across. Then she froze.

She staggered. I grabbed her around the shoulders. She was dizzy, she told me. She knew she would fall.

"Call your pony," I shouted. Immediately he came galloping through the air, swooping in like Pegasus on wings, and lifted us both into the sky. As we soared up to the clouds, I sensed her relief.

Now she could look down and describe all she saw with great enthusiasm. She felt no fear at this height; in fact, she felt liberated.

We flew above gorgeous snow-capped mountains. Josephine kept pointing things out to me: a river that sparkled in the sunlight, a distant village, an eagle gliding below us. She took it all in. She seemed somehow to be at home here.

Then she tensed. She took a deep breath. I heard her say something, but it came out as a mumble. She pointed at a waterfall. Billows of misty spray rose from its base. I wondered whether it was connected with the bridge. "I must go there," she said.

"I'm with you. Let's go!"

The pony descended rapidly, taking us directly down toward the waterfall.

"Oh, my God!" Josephine began to sob uncontrollably.

I opened my eyes and looked at her body where it lay on the floor, next to the fireplace.

"They're going to kill him," she said, trying to fight back the sobs. Her body was stiff as a board.

"Who is he?"

"Me." The way she said it sent a chill up my spine. "They are going to sacrifice me to the waterfall."

"Why?"

"Because they think the waterfall requires it. Or else the river will flood their village, my village."

"Who are they?"

"Men from my village. Five of them. All painted in black and red stripes. Down their chests and legs. One has a huge club and keeps threatening to knock my head in with it." She reached up and touched the top of her head, the precise spot where I had seen the dark energy mass.

I realized that Josephine had entered the parallel world of an earlier life. Past-life regression, as it is generally called in our society, is not un-common in shamanic healing. I asked, "Why you?"

She hesitated. I watched her lips move and understood that she was asking them. "Because I'm thirty-five and haven't yet killed an enemy." The recollection that the acrophobia had become debilitating when Josephine turned thirty-five hit me like a stone to the gut. I felt sweat break out on my forehead.

She was quiet. I knew the pony had taken her close to the scene. "What's happening?" I asked.

"They've shoved me to the edge of the cliff. I can feel the spray from way down there. We're about even with the top of the waterfall across the gorge." Her body convulsed. Both hands flew up to shield the top of her head.

"What?"

"That man's club!"

"Stop it," I said as calmly as I could, softening the drum. "Freeze the scene right there and stay with it. I'm going to do a soul retrieval. Can you hold it right there? Can you wait?"

"Yes," she said, her voice quivering.

I called on my wolf. Together we journeyed into a dark, forbidding realm. We had made similar visits before, yet I never liked them. I always felt nervous and apprehensive while we were here. I called out for the part of Josephine's soul that had fled during that moment on the cliff. The weight of the place was oppressive. Breathing was becoming difficult.

I heard a tiny voice. The wolf wagged her tail and, racing up a steep, dark tunnel, led me to a small boy. Huddled in the blackness of the place, the child looked terrified. I explained who we were and invited him to return with us. He immediately relaxed. His expression showed relief. I told him that before he could do that he would have to help us deal with the trauma that had caused him to come here. I asked whether he could handle that. He took my hand and, with a smile, assured me he could. I hugged the wolf's neck and, holding the child's hand, was carried swiftly out of the oppressive place.

I saw Josephine lying on the floor. Without hesitating, I camayed the little boy into her. An instantaneous sigh came from her, along with a momentary grin.

"Does the waterfall require a sacrifice?" I asked.

"Yes," she replied. "But . . ." There was a long pause. "It doesn't have to be a person."

"What then?"

She smiled. "Flowers."

"Explain that to those men."

A long moment of silence. "They don't believe me. And they want to know what you're doing here."

"Tell them," I said in a voice grown so husky that I barely recognized it as my own, "that I'm here to save your life. Tell them I will kill them if they don't obey." The words seemed to come from someone other than me; hearing them sent a shudder through my body. "What are they doing?" I asked after a short pause.

"Nothing. Just standing there. They seem unsure of themselves. The man who was going to strike my head with the club has moved back. The club is at his side. He looks docile." She let a breath out slowly.

"Give them flowers," I commanded. "Tell them to throw the flowers to the waterfall. It is all that is required."

Her hands wiggled at her sides. "I am picking the flowers myself. Orange and blue petals. Beautiful flowers that grow along the cliff. The men are watching. One of them—the one with the club—says they will do as I have told them to. Okay. They are accepting the flowers. Smelling them. They are raising them above their heads, making a sort of ceremony out of it, and now—throwing them to the waterfall." She squirmed, rolling slightly onto her side. I noticed a slight smile. "They are laughing. They want me to return to the village with them."

"Tell them to go on alone. You will come later. Wait. Thank them for their help. Thank them for appeasing the waterfall and saving your village."

Her lips moved, as before. "Good-bye," she said.

"Now," I continued, quickening the drum beat as I talked, "ask the pony to take us home. The part of your soul that fled is back. You have taken care of the trauma." I felt a tremendous sense of relief. "You have changed the dream of your memory. From now on everything will be different."

Several months later, Josephine and I were in the Amazon with Raul and fourteen other people. By the time Josephine reached the bridge, everyone in the group knew her story. Many of the participants were psychologists, who took more than an idle interest in her case. The fact that she had tested herself in glass elevators and on ladders before leaving the States, as well as in volcano craters and small airplanes in Ecuador, had merited documentation in their journals. They were impressed that she had gone so long without a sign of acrophobia. But the real test was the bridge itself.

I stood there on the step leading to the bridge with the rest of them. Deep inside, I felt assured, but I was curious to see how confident she would be. And there was always the possibility . . . , but I refused to give energy to the negative.

She sauntered up the path, her arms swinging nonchalantly at her sides, a big smile across her face, aware that every eye followed her. We stepped aside, giving her plenty of room to see the bridge. She stood and looked at it. Her hands rose to her hips; her posture was downright arrogant. "Yes," I said to myself. "Yes, Josephine, play it for all it's worth."

She started forward, then froze. I could feel the people around me grow tense. I followed her eyes down to the river. There in the gorge below, the water seethed like an angry god. The thought crossed my mind that it needed a sacrifice. I threw it a mental flower. A long log swept down the river, struck a submerged rock, and leapt high into the air. Someone gasped. The log landed in the rapids and was snatched by the current to continue its journey toward the Atlantic Ocean.

When I looked back at the bridge, I could not believe my eyes. Josephine was a quarter of the way across. She was dancing, an odd combination of jig and skip. And she was singing. Her clear voice sounded absolutely euphoric. She moved quickly and without any fear whatsoever. It took her no time to reach the other side. The rest of us broke into loud applause.

She jumped up and down, her hands held together over her head like a victorious prizefighter. Then, to our collective amazement, she started back across. This time she did not dance, but rather walked briskly, her laughing eyes on us. When she arrived to within a couple of yards of the bank where we stood, she stopped. "What are you waiting for?" she asked. She turned abruptly and headed back across the bridge. Her right arm swept the air in a motion for us to follow. "Come on!"

11

Dream Change

The crater in Cuicocha Volcano is so deep that local legend says it reaches to the very center of Pachamama. As you sit on the side of the crater, you look down into an azure lake that fills all but the last three hundred feet or so. Just beyond is the sacred mountain, Grandmother Cotacachi. Magnificent as it rises into the sky beyond the water, Cotacachi dwarfs the impressive mountain on the rim of whose crater you sit. You know that you are in the presence of a living entity. You understand why the spirit of Cotacachi is invoked by Manco, Iyarina, and the other shamans in the northern Andes. It is far grander and more powerful than European cathedrals, Egyptian pyramids, Mayan temples, the World Trade Center, or any other edifice built by the human community.

When you sit on the rock outcroppings and look across the lake at the great spire, you feel empowered. Struck by a sense of déjà vu, you realize that it comes from the knowledge that people have experienced this same feeling at this very place for a long time. The power this mountain has given to human beings goes back many thousands of years, to a time long before the birth of the man whose name would be invoked by the Spanish conquistadors in their attempt to wipe out the Pachamama-honoring spirituality and the shamanic healing techniques indigenous to this region.

On a day after one of my groups had returned to the United States, I traveled up to the lake at Cuicocha. Clouds drifted around the summit of Cotacachi, like spirits weaving their magic. They took me back to the group, to dreamed memories of our times together with the Otavalan, Colorado, Salasacan, and Shuar shamans. I could see and feel each participant, now back home, and knew that each one felt the presence of the group, each had been changed, empowered.

I walked up the steep trail along the edge of the crater, aware that I was following in the footsteps of great healers who had gained my deepest respect. It is to these mountains—to Cuicocha, Cotacachi, Imbabura, Cotopaxi, Cayambi, and Chimborazo—that they come for strength and enlightenment. It is here that they wander in search of sacred stones and other huacas, here that they are visited by spirit guides and power animals.

I began to climb a shoulder of Cotacachi. Around me, butterflies flitted in the deep grasses, invisible birds called back and forth, and an occasional grasshopper startled the tranquillity with a sudden leap into the sparkling air. The sun mesmerized me. I lay down to bask in its soft heat.

Feeling Pachamama beneath me, I watched the wispy clouds play around Cotacachi's summit. My thoughts drifted to Manco, Kitiar, and my other teachers. I closed my eyes and moved through a few of the worlds whose magical doors they had helped open. I felt honored to be a part of this world and those worlds, their worlds. I felt a great love for them and also a contentment with my responsibility to share that love with others of my generation, as well as generations to come. I felt peaceful and, at the same time, aware of my oneness with Pachamama, Inti, Mama Kilya, and those three pillars—as Candelaria had described them back at the Katalysis board meeting—of plant, animal, and mineral.

Then I knew that I was not alone. I felt her presence even before I heard the soft melody of her song coming toward me.

I sat up and, to my great delight, saw Iyarina ascending the path. When she spied me, she stopped. She cocked her head to the side, as if seeing me from a different angle would help solve the mystery of my being there. Her face broke into a grin. I stood and shook her hand, wondering at the youthful energy that radiated from her. I had not seen her for several months. Somehow she had shed years; it was difficult to believe what I knew to be fact: that she had at least five great-grandchildren. Without speaking, she sat in the grass next to the place where I had lain and motioned for me to join her.

Her voice continued to sound like the song she had been singing. She inquired about some of the people I had taken to her for healings during my previous trips.

I told her that all had improved after seeing her. She was pleased to hear this. I described in detail a telephone conversation I had had several weeks earlier with a woman healed by her of a serious intestinal problem. She nodded slowly, as though she had anticipated every word I said.

Then, without giving it much thought, I related to her the incident that had happened those many months before, when Raul and I had taken a group to her house and, not finding her there, had moved on to Manco's. Although I had seen her since, it had always been with a group, and I had not had the opportunity to talk privately with her. Now I shared the entire experience, including the bonding that had occurred between Manco and me and the wisdom I had gained over the ensuing weeks. I especially emphasized the dream work we had done together and the techniques for dream change he had taught me.

Her eyes lingered on mine for what seemed a long time. I thought she herself had left this world for another. At last, she smiled. Then she told me the most extraordinary story.

One of her inner pilot guides had warned her that we were on our way to her home that day, and had also told her that she was not meant to work with us, that something else was in store for us. It was because of this message that she had left—telling no one, not even her husband, of her reasons.

"You see," she said, looking directly into my eyes, "that was a very important moment for us, for me as well as you, a time of transition and learning."

"So you knew all along? You gave up the opportunity to work with a lot of wealthy gringo clients?" I could not resist a chuckle. "It doesn't sound too wise."

She looked across the crater at Cotacachi. "Well," she replied, "your clients were in good hands, weren't they?" The grandmother mountain's reflection in the azure water gave the impression of two Cotacachis, one ascending to the heavens, the other reaching down into the heart of Pachamama.

We sat in silence. A flock of birds flew overhead. A wind from off the lake rippled the grassy slope. Time stood still.

Then Iyarina turned to me. "Manco is a very old person. His knowledge is deeper than the crater," she said, pointing into the lake. Her hands rose in an arc above us. "It transcends all you can see, all you hear, feel, smell, or taste. He is older than the oldest saint." She stood up. Wiping twigs and dust from her skirt, she looked about. I felt that she was taking everything in with each of the senses she had just listed and also with the "other" senses I had come to appreciate. "What you have learned about dreaming is meaningless unless you and your people use it."

I rose to my feet and took her hand in mine. Our eyes met. "The dream," she said, "is everything." Her fingers squeezed mine. She smiled, turned, and headed down the trail.

Epilogue

Cars hurtled past. I felt trapped in a nightmare of blaring horns, surrounded by whirling steel-and-glass monsters, alone and completely out of place. I swerved to avoid a broken tailpipe in the middle of my lane and was nearly sideswiped by a huge truck. Its angry horn echoed down the highway. A fist emerged from the truck's window, a solitary protruding finger.

Once again I was driving north on Interstate 95, from Miami to Palm Beach County, returning from a trip to Ecuador with a group of university students. This time I was not fleeing the threat of violent riots. I was simply going home.

I reached down to turn on the radio, then stopped, recalling the announcer's voice from that other time. I could not remember the exact words, only that he had been discussing justice in the United States, something about the dreams of the Founding Fathers.

I glanced through the side window at the Miami skyline, then quickly back at the road. I was feeling the culture shock that I had felt so many times before, and the repulsion for what we have done to our Mother in the name of progress, as well as the future we are creating for my daughter, Jessica, and for our other children, as well as for the birds, animals, reptiles, insects, plants, trees, flowers, mountains, oceans, deserts, forests, and rocks.

Then I saw Kitiar's face. His ancient eyes sparkled. I heard his tumank. Somewhere, deep down inside, I was aware of a strong sense of hope.

I had seen people change. Numi had told me to bring people who wanted to learn so that the shamans could help us create new dreams. I had witnessed the resulting power. I had seen materialism stripped from people, had watched them become newly enamored with Pachamama. I had witnessed medical doctors and business executives who had invested their lives and millions of dollars in money-driven careers suddenly dedicating themselves to the spiritual ideals of a philosophy that previously they would have shrugged off as primitive or naive. I had hiked with scientists, psychologists, teachers, lawyers, and college students through snowfields in the high Andes and deep into the Amazon rain forests, had held their hands in circles around huaca-enshrined fires, joined them in chants led by head-hunting warriors, helped them through the ordeals of ayahuasca. I understood the profundity of their transformations.

Dream change worked. Of that I had no doubt. In less than two years of taking people to the shamans and of workshops in the United States, I had accumulated a wealth of information and testimonials from a multitude of personalities from varying professions, and all of it served witness to the power of the dream.

In his book *In the Absence of the Sacred,* Jerry Mander says:

> It has proven unfortunate for the survival of Indian nations that their way of viewing the world is so drastically at odds with the views of American technological society. Indigenous systems of logic have not led them to emphasize expansion, power, or high-impact technologies of violence. Meanwhile, several aspects of the industrial system, especially in capitalist societies, do celebrate and even require the goals of expansion, growth, and exploitation and the development of the technologies appropriate to those goals. When the two worldviews come into conflict, we in the industrial cultures have the brute advantage of the violent technologies to help wipe out indigenous cultures; we then interpret this so-called victory as further evidence of our greater fitness to survive.*

Driving up Interstate 95, I began to see another side to what Mander says. The difference between indigenous and Western worldviews has indeed been unfortunate for the survival of Indian nations. Yet the persistence of those indigenous views is fortunate, for therein lies our best hope for the survival of the human species. That hope is a seed that has taken root in fertile indigenous cosmologies and Earth-honoring dreams, enabling us to re-dream, to re-create, ourselves. We all have the ability to become Birdmen and to empower ourselves, our societies, our species, to adapt. What we in the technological cultures have lacked is faith in those abilities and the will to act, to employ our powers and channel them into efforts that will benefit all three pillars. The shamans are now rising from the mists of time, springing like trees from that potent seed, in order to teach us about ourselves, our powers, and our need to create ourselves anew.

A billboard flashed past; like so many others along this stretch of Interstate 95, it enticed the traveler to purchase a "dream" home bordering one of the more than a thousand golf courses in Florida. On the plane I had read a magazine article in which the author cited examples of the

---

*Jerry Mander, *In the Absence of the Sacred: The Failure of Technology and the Survival of the Indian Nations* (San Francisco: Sierra Club Books, 1991), p. 220.

massive destruction caused by golf courses and their insecticides and fertilizers—all to benefit less than 10 percent of our population. He then went on to state: "It wasn't always this way. Before Porsches and polyester, golf was an unpretentious, working-class game from Scotland that conformed itself to nature, not the other way around."*

Once again I wondered about my culture. Why do we have this compulsion to take what is beautiful in nature and alter it? Who are these individuals who think they can outsmart God? What is it in our society that encourages such egotistical beliefs?

These questions took my thoughts to Thomas Berry, a philosopher and priest who has influenced a generation of environmentalists. He too had just returned from Ecuador—two weeks ahead of me. While there he had asked questions similar to my own.

Shortly after publication in 1992 of Berry's *The Universe Story* (coauthored with the physicist Brian Swimme), I had been asked to speak at a celebration honoring him. I had taken that occasion to invite him to visit the shamans. Not only had he accepted, but he had also taught a course in Ecuador to my university students. It was from this trip that I was now returning, and I found myself looking to Berry for the answers to one of the questions my hectic ride up Interstate 95 was raising.

"This compulsion," Thomas Berry had written,

> to use, to consume, has found its ultimate expression in our own times, when the ideal is to take the natural resources from the earth and transform them by industrial processes for consumption by a society that lives on ever-heightened rates of consumption. That consumption has something sacred about it is obvious from the central position it now occupies. This is all quite clear from the relentless advertising campaigns designed to convince society that there is neither peace nor joy, neither salvation nor paradise, except through heightened consumption.†

My attention was drawn to the side of the highway again, where a parade of billboards promised that paradise, if only the traveler would purchase this or consume that. It was obvious that someone out there—some group—was fully aware of the power of the dream and was using that power to channel an entire population's subconscious aspirations.

---

*Bruce Selcraig, "Greens Fees: Whose Eagles? Whose Birdies? Nature Pays a Price for our Love Affair with Golf" (*Sierra*, July/August 1993, Vol. 78/No.4, p. 71).

†Brain Swimme and Thomas Berry, *The Universe Story* (San Francisco: Harper San Francisco, 1992), p. 73.

These people were playing the roles shamans play in other cultures. Unlike Kitiar, Manco, Iyarina, and the other Ecuadoran shamans with whom I worked, however, they were not using their powers in Earth-honoring ways. Rather than trying to restore the balance between humans and nature, they were doing everything possible to further disrupt that balance. They met the classic definition of shamans in that they used the power of the subconscious, along with physical reality, to effect change. Yet by no stretch of the imagination were they healers. They were effecting change not for the good of others or of society as a whole, but only in order to satisfy their own personal greed.

I thought about people I had met at workshops and traveled with to the Andes and Amazon, people who had learned to dream new dreams. They had changed, had done complete about-faces in a short time. I again heard the soft voice of Thomas Berry:

> We need to remember that this process whereby we invent ourselves in these cultural modes is guided by visionary experiences that come to us in some transitional process from the inner shaping tendencies that we carry within us, often in revelatory dream experience. Such dream experiences are so universal and so important in the psychic life of the individual and of the community that techniques of dreaming are taught in some societies.

Images of Manco flashed before me as he guided me through the steps of dream change. I could see him sitting right in front of me, yet at the same time I was cognizant of the road, the traffic, and my need to concentrate on driving. Kitiar appeared next to Manco, and I remembered the night a week earlier when he had offered ayahuasca to the group of university students.

Raul, Rosa, and I had taken pains to explain to Kitiar that the students were prohibited from using psychotropic plants—at least as long as they were enrolled in the university's program. This prohibition had been difficult for him to accept, since plants—along with their human allies, the shamans—are considered by the Shuar to be essential to the educational process. He had given us a rather dubious smile and agreed that, although it was a strange custom, he would try to work with the students, try to help them separate dreams from fantasies and make their dreams come true, try to heal them, without administering ayahuasca. "I will take it myself," he had concluded with a nod. "I will do much of their work for them."

I feared that I must appear to Kitiar like another white missionary who had come not to learn but to impose the value system of my culture on him and his people. To his credit, he did not seem to see it this way. He had patted me reassuringly on the shoulder, moved forward with the ceremony, and completed half a dozen powerful healing journeys with the students that night. At the end, in a touching gesture of friendship, he had presented me with his tumank and a promise to teach me how to play it.

"What we seem unwilling or unable to recognize," writes Thomas Berry, "is that our entire modern world is itself inspired not by any rational process, but by a distorted dream experience, perhaps by the most powerful dream that has ever taken possession of human imagination. Our sense of progress, our entire technological society, however rational in its functioning, is a pure dream vision in its origins and in its objectives."

I looked out at the massive buildings that line the coast of Florida, and I understood that the foundations for our dreamings have been laid by a few individuals. Every culture has such people. In the Western world, those individuals have given voice to dreams that have now manifested themselves all around us, in the billboards, the traffic, the heavy industries, and in our fixation on perpetual mining and construction. We have all bought into the philosophies behind those manifestations and, in so doing, given energy to the dreams of those individuals. As Numi pointed out, the dreams have come true, and we are now beginning to understand their nightmarish implications.

How, I wondered as I drove past a parcel of barren land where a forest had recently been cleared to make room for yet another shopping mall, would a true shaman view this fixation on construction? I thought I heard Manco's voice.

"It is not construction that is the problem, nor mining, nor any other activity or profession," he seemed to say. "It is the goal of these, the dreamed result."

What I saw outside my car window was not the work of malicious human beings determined to destroy the planet. It was, rather, the result of a set of values, a cookbook of working philosophies, that has grown out of the dreams of a handful of individuals who espoused utopian theories of individual enlightenment, freedom, and rights to accumulate property. Those philosophies have been warped over time, stretched and contracted, molded and co-opted by greedy people who have converted the original dreams into justifications for gluttony and personal aggrandizement.

The real question, then, is, How can we turn those philosophies around; how can we re-dream our position in the natural world? As I passed a road crew at work, it suddenly became apparent that the only workable answer rested in emphasizing what we do best.

Construction. I spied the stacks of Florida Power and Light Company's plant and remembered the discourse I had held with myself five weeks earlier. Construction is the thing we excel at; promoting and protecting it drives our educational, commercial, political, social, and judicial systems. To change the dream will require a change in our attitude toward construction.

Words like *durable, guaranteed,* and *built to last* came to mind, words that had been etched into my mind by years of conditioning. I thought about the meaning of *construction* to the Shuar. It meant building a house that was intended to last only a few years; after that the house would be allowed to dissolve back into the Earth and a new one would be constructed somewhere else. It meant erecting a small dam for catching fish, which would be torn down before sunset. It meant a hammock made from vines, a blowgun of chonta wood and beeswax, a dugout canoe. The concept of constructing something "durable" was foreign to the Shuar, and to all tribal people. You did not want a thing to last; you wanted it to serve a specific, short-term purpose and then return to nature. How different their dream from the one I had been taught!

I realized that our entire economy revolves around what we think of as "heavy" industry and "durable" goods, and that this is completely contrary to the natural world and those who live close to it. In nature, and among traditional societies, nothing is durable; everything is in flux. While our historians consider a bronze arrowhead to be superior to a wooden one, Núnkui and Pachamama would not agree; the wooden one is superior because it is less durable. The same could be said for pottery, and for everything else that we make, shape, or mold.

When politicians run for office, they talk about "growing" the economy. What they usually mean is building things that last, manufacturing houses, cars, appliances, computers, and other products from cement, metal, plastic, and other raw materials that are mined from Pachamama and that pass certain standards of endurance. The production of these things consumes vast amounts of energy and causes unquantifiable pollution. Ultimately, the things themselves create huge trash piles that are incompatible with the land and water surrounding them. How different this dream from that of an Amazonian tribe!

I knew as I watched the steel-and-glass high rises glide by that my culture was not about to return to a hunting and gathering lifestyle. So, I asked myself, what sort of dream *can* we create? It had to be one that honors the Earth above all else and that is not dependent on the violent technologies we have come to associate with mining and constructing.

My thoughts wandered to the people who join me in my workshops and trips. Most of them share my feelings in this regard, yet they are people who must earn money to feed and clothe their families. Many are far removed from mining and construction. They are psychologists, doctors, chiropractors, dancers, massage therapists, health food and book store owners, nurses, writers, musicians, and poets. Perhaps herein lies the key. Why sell each other durable goods when we can sell each other ones that dissolve into thin air? Would not the economy be much better off—and politicians just as happy—if everything we sold each other, except for a few essentials, were "soft" instead of "hard" and "built *not* to last"?

Many of the psychologists and other therapists who study with me say that their techniques for helping others have been changed by psychonavigation, dream change, and shamanism. One confided that she now accomplishes in two sessions what previously had taken five or six. When I apologized for cutting back her income, she only laughed. "On the contrary," she said, "the number of clients coming to me has tripled. Word spreads quickly!" A medical doctor admits that, in diagnosing, he now pays greater attention to his own intuitions. "I understand," he told me, "that my feelings about my patients often provide better information than the computer readouts. In the process, I have become a more sensitive human being."

One example of a proactive and creative approach is Earth Dream Alliance (EDA)—a nonprofit organization that sprouted from the dreams of people who joined my trips and are committed to changing consciousness throughout the world so that the communal human dream will become more Earth-honoring. An EDA objective is to purchase and conserve forest lands on behalf of indigenous people and to help these people establish shamanic learning centers, where participants from many cultures can exchange information. EDA encourages people to clothe and feed their families through such sustainable activities as the production and marketing of naturally renewable products. It also organizes workshops and trips to the shamans.

Other examples of "softer," Earth-honoring approaches to making a living are becoming increasingly familiar, ranging from for-profit corporations, such as Shaman Pharmaceuticals, Inc., to organic farms. Yet these are still only examples, not the norm. They are not enough. Every one of us must alter our dream, must continually re-create ourselves and the societies we form. Loving our Mother is not a one-time decision. It is an everlasting, minute-by-minute commitment. We must journey deep into our own hearts, rescue our dreams from the clutches of the public relations people, and become Birdmen. We must plant the seed, water it every day, and take pride in the beauty it creates.

Looking out the car window, I realized that there are many ways to "construct." We in the so-called civilized world have defined that activity in the narrowest of terms. Surely we can break through those barriers and expand our definition to include endeavors that respond to a more compassionate dream. In doing this we will be moving ourselves down a path to hope, not along that old highway to the abyss. It is up to each of us to decide as an individual, and up to all of us to decide as a species, that we no longer want to travel the route to that place Lame Deer described as the "big, empty hole."

Ahead on Interstate 95 a bulldozer was backing down a ramp off a flatbed truck. My thoughts returned to a night in the Amazon rain forest. I heard Kitiar's violin and watched a bulldozer pushing walls to the distant horizon. I understood that the bulldozer can be used not only to flatten trees but also to push back the limits of our knowledge and open the way into patterns of understanding that are not confined by the walls of history. It all depends on how we dream it.

Glossary

Arútam. Shuar spirit, proctector and guide for men. Contacting Arútam requires fasting, trekking to the sacred waterfall, and undergoing a vision quest (usually accompanied by a shaman and involving ayahuasca).

Ayahuasca. Quechua word that is often translated in Spanish as "vine of the soul," "vine of death," "vine of enlightenment," or "vine of spirit wisdom"; also known as *natem* (Shuar), *yaje*, and *caapi*. Its scientific name is *Banisteriopsis caapi*, a member of the Malpighiaceae family, containing a group of alkaloids known as betacarbolines, of which harmine is the primary component. A psychotropic vine revered throughout the Amazon and Andes as a sacred plant that enables the user to communicate directly with Pachamama, the natural world of plants, animals, minerals, and the supernatural world. Ayahuasca is considered to be a ladder into a higher level where the individual experiences unity with all else, oneness with the universal dream. Prepared by boiling, usually with other plants.

Ayumpum. Shuar god who was sent by Etsáa to teach people how to boil and use ayahuasca.

Camay. Quechua word that is difficult to translate into Spanish, English, and other Indo-European–based languages, since it connotes the process of blowing spirit, soul, the unity of all things into someone or something; translations include "animating or breathing spirit into an object" and "giving life, sustenance."* The process by which the god-creator Viracocha created the dream that became the universe. Technique employed by shamans to blow balance, unity, and health into people, plants, and minerals; also used in shamanic retrievals, including power animal, inner pilot, and soul retrievals. *Camay* is the more connom term among Peruvian Quechua speakers; Ecuadoran Quechua speakers are more likely to use *fucquay*.

---

*Regina Harrison, *Signs, Songs, and Memory in the Andes: Translating Quechua Language and Culture* (Austin: University of Texas Press, 1989), pp. 76, 224.

Cañaris. A Quechua-speaking people of the Ecuadoran highlands north of Cuenca; reputed to have offered the fiercest resistance to Incan invaders, and still considered to be highly resistant to change.

Chankin. Shuar term for basket.

Chicha. An alcoholic beverage, often translated in Spanish as "beer," prepared in the Amazon and Andes by fermentation of various fruits, tubers, and herbs. (South American peoples produced alcoholic beverages long before Columbus's arrival.) Shuar women produce large quantities of chicha every day by chewing and spitting manioc (yuca) and allowing the resulting liquid to ferment overnight or—for more strength—several days. Chicha is an extremely important element of Shuar ritual and diet; only women are allowed to make it and to serve it during the welcoming ceremonies when guests arrive at a Shuar home. The Shuar consume vast amounts of it; chicha is sometimes compared to the potato or rice in that it provides essential carbohydrates, calories, and starches.

Chonta. A type of fruit palm (*Guilielma speciosa,* Bactris Gasipaes) noted for its extreme hardness and durability, used to make spears, knives, and blowguns; the fruit is made into a special chicha by the Shuar and is the focal point for an important celebration and annual festival.

Colorados. An indigenous people living on the western slopes of Ecuador's Andes, famous for their use of red dyes in their hair and the healing powers of their shamans.

Cotacachi. The powerful mother or grandmother volcano of Imbabura Province, Ecuador. Held in high esteem as a sacred healing force by the Otavalan shamans, often invoked during their healings and traveled to during psychonavigational journeys. Consort to and female energy balance for Imbabura, the male mountain across the valley, a valley in which many of the most highly respected shamans live.

Cotopaxi. World's highest active volcano, just south of the equator in Ecuador, perpetually covered by glaciers and snow; considered sacred by many indigenous people and often invoked during shamanic healings. As predicted in an ancient legend long before Columbus's arrival, it erupted on the day the last Incan king, Atahuellpa, was killed (by the Spanish conquistador Pizarro).

Etsáa. Shuar god of the sun; he once lived on earth with the Shuar and is the subject of many myths and legends.

Huaca. Quechua word for a sacred place or object. Often used in reference to the stones, plants, and other items shamans employ in their ceremonies and for healings and psychonavigational travels; shamanic huacas frequently come from sacred places such as Cotacachi, Imbabura, and Cotopaxi.

Huaoranis (or **Waoranis**).   An indigenous people of the Ecuadoran Amazon whose nomadic lifestyle has recently been disrupted by U.S. and other oil companies.

Imbabura.   The powerful father or grandfather mountain, located just north of the equator and across the valley from his consort, Cotacachi, in Imbabura Province, Ecuador. The male balance to the female energy of Cotacachi, often invoked by Otavalan shamans, who consider people living between the two mountains to be endowed with a special knowledge of the supernatural.

Inti.   Quechua word for the sun or sun god; according to Incan cosmology, gold was Inti's sweat and was entrusted to people not to be used for material purposes but rather to be safeguarded as one of the threads woven into the dream of Inti, Pachamama, and Mama Kilya.

Iyarina.   Quechua word for the concept of remembering.

Jémpe.   Shuar god who maintains balance between the male and female; symbolized by the hummingbird.

Kenkuim.   Shuar term for "turtle."

Kitiar.   A Shuar violin, usually carved from a single block of wood.

Lowland Quichuas.   An indigenous people of the Ecuadoran Amazon, considered by other Amazonian peoples to possess invisible darts of great shamanic power.

Mama Kilya.   In Quechua, the moon or moon goddess; according to Incan cosmology, silver was Mama Kilya's teardrops and was entrusted to people not to be used for material purposes but rather to be safeguarded as one of the threads woven into the dream of Mama Kilya, Pachamama, and Inti.

Mati.   Small gourd used by the Shuar as part of the quiver for blowgun darts.

Nase.   Shuar term for the wind that travels through the forests blowing balance into all things, a healing wind that symbolizes the unifying dream.

Numi.   Shuar word for "tree" or "pole."

Núnkui.   Shuar goddess of the earth, of plants and gardens, protector of women; she resides in the earth during the day, healing the soil and working with roots, and rises above the ground at night to dance with the plants, animals, and people.

Otavalans.   An indigenous people living just north of the equator, mostly in Imbabura Province, Ecuador, between Cotacachi and Imbabura; famous for their skills as musicians, weavers, and especially shamans; a prosperous people who, despite their material success, have maintained their traditional values and lifestyle. Part of the Quechua-speaking group.

Pachamama. Quechua for "Mother Earth," "Mother Universe," or "Universal Mother"; the Earth, goddess of the Earth, the place where Inti's sweat (gold) and Mama Kilya's tears (silver) are woven into the universal dream.

Psychonavigation. A body of techniques for navigating through the psyche (soul, spirit, collective unconscious) to a place where one needs to be (physically, mentally, emotionally, psychologically, or spiritually); used throughout the world for shamanic journeying, healing, and to obtain guidance in decision making and creativity.

Quechua. A language and also a word used to refer to people who speak it. Millions of Andean people today speak one of the dialects of this language, which was spread by the Incas from what is now northern Chile into parts of Peru, Bolivia, and Ecuador. Concepts expressed in Quechua, especially as they relate to spirituality, psychonavigation, and other shamanic practices, are very different from the Judeo-Christian ones introduced by the Spanish conquistadors and missionaries; for this reason, many Quechua words cannot be translated accurately into either Spanish or English. In such cases, throughout this book, rather than trying to apply an English equivalent, the Quechua has been used, along with a description of the meaning. Quechua, as it is currently spoken, is by no means uniform. In Ecuador it varies so significantly from the Peruvian form that it is often referred to as Quichua. Despite differences in pronunciation and vocabulary, however, many of the concepts are standard throughout the Andes. For the sake of both simplicity and consistency, this book generally uses the Quechua form as it has been incorporated into the Official Alphabet of 1975 (revised in 1983 by the First Workshop for the Writing System of Quechua and Aymara), although this may not be the form actually used by the particular speaker or his indigenous group.*

Quipu camayoc. Quechua for "those who *camay* [breath unity, soul, spirit, and life] into the *quipus* [knotted strings carried by runners throughout the Incan Empire]." Since the quipus contained coded information about crops, wars, laws, and other things vital to the empire, the quipu camayoc was really an interpreter of messages, an extremely important and highly skilled individual who carried a great deal of responsibility and power.

---

*For a more detailed and highly stimulating discussion, see Regina Harrison, *Signs, Songs, and Memory in the Andes: Translating Quechua Language and Culture* (Austin: University of Texas Press, 1989).

Salasacans.   An indigenous people who live on the eastern slopes of the Andes in an area that provides a transition from the high Andes to the Amazon; they practice a form of shamanic healing using guinea pigs that reflects their origins in Bolivia. The Salasacans were defeated by the Incas and, as part of a pacification program, were moved from their home in Bolivia to Ecuador. Part of the Quechua-speaking group.

Sangay.   An extremely active volcano located in the eastern Andes on the edge of the Amazon Basin.

Secha.   Shuar name for a brilliantly colored bird.

Shaman.   Title originally from Central Asia that today is widely used in place of "medicine man," "wizard," "sorcerer," or "witch doctor" for a man or woman who journeys into the Dreamtime or parallel worlds and uses the subconscious, along with physical reality, to effect change; a psychonavigator who uses his or her powers to change people, plants, and the weather and to divine the future; may use plants and herbal medicines, along with spiritual healings.

Shuar.   An indigenous people living in the western Amazon Basin, mostly along the Cutucú Mountain range, east of the Andes, in Ecuador and Peru and the territories where the borders between the two countries are still contested; famous in former times for their ferocity in fighting and their shrunken-head trophies; noted today for the power of their shamans and the use of ayahuasca. They speak their own language, also called Shuar. Sometimes referred to as *Jivaro*.

Suntai.   Shuar term for a type of iguana.

Tantar.   Shield used by the Shuar in battle.

Trago.   A strong alcoholic drink made from sugar cane; crystal clear, it is considered very pure—a direct link with spirits of the plant world—and is used by shamans throughout the Andes and Amazon for cleansings, purification, camaying, and creating fire.

Tsúnkqui.   Shuar goddess of the waters who is also considered to have been the first shaman; she rides on a turtle, and as a result turtle stools ("chumpis") have become symbols for shamans as well as for her; protected by crocodiles and anacondas.

Tumank.   Shuar musical instrument made by tying a string of monkey gut or fishing line from one end to the other of a three- to four-foot-long bowed bamboo stick; held between the lips while the string is plucked with the fingers, it emits a beautiful, delicate sound that has been likened to falling water and singing spirits.

Tuntiak.   Shuar name for the rainbow in the sacred waterfall; according to Shuar legend, the first man and woman emerged from Tuntiak, at the same instant and equal.

Wirikuta. Sacred place for the Huichol people of Central Mexico, an indigenous group that is famous for its vibrant tapestries, often made with the help of peyote. Each year Huichol shamans lead their people on pilgrimages to Wirikuta; retracing the steps of the ancient ones who wove the original dream, the pilgrims weave together the tapestry of life and reaffirm their unity with the rest of the natural world and with the original dream itself.

Yampún. Shuar term for "parrot."

Bibliography

Alexander, F. *Psychosomatic Medicine*. New York: Norton, 1950.

Allison, J. "Respiration changes during transcendental meditation." *Lancet* 1 (1970): 833–34.

Andrews, L. *Jaguar Woman and the Wisdom of the Butterfly Tree*. San Francisco: Harper and Row, 1986.

Bach, R. *Illusions: The Adventures of a Reluctant Messiah*. New York: Dell, 1977.

Benson, H. *Beyond the Relaxation Response*. New York: Times Books, 1984.

———. *The Relaxation Response*. New York: Morrow, 1975.

Berry, T. *The Dream of the Earth*. San Francisco: Sierra Club Books, 1988.

Blair, Lawrence, with Lorne Blair. *Ring of Fire: An Indonesian Odyssey*. Rochester, Vt.: Park Street Press, 1991.

Bower, B. "Shaping up your mind." *Science News* 126 (August 2, 1986): 75.

Brennan, B. A. *Hands of Light: A Guide to Healing through the Human Energy Field*. New York: Bantam Books, 1988.

Capra, F. *The Tao of Physics*. New York: Bantam Books, 1988.

Carey, K. *Return of the Bird Tribes*. San Francisco: Harper San Francisco, 1988.

Castañeda, C. *The Eagle's Gift*. New York: Simon and Shuster, 1981.

———. *The Teachings of Don Juan: A Yaqui Way of Knowledge*. Berkeley and Los Angeles: University of California Press, 1968.

Chang, C. Y. *Creativity and Taoism*. New York: Julian Press, 1963.

Chatwin, B. *The Songlines*. New York: Penguin Books, 1988.

Chopra, D. *Quantum Healing: Exploring the Frontiers of Mind/Body Medicine*. New York: Bantam Books, 1990.

Colby, B. N., and L. M. Colby. *The Daykeeper: The Life and Discourse of an Ixil Diviner*. Cambridge, Mass.: Harvard University Press, 1981.

Cowan, J. *Mysteries of the Dream-Time: The Spiritual Life of Australian Aborigines*. Bridgeport, England: Prism Press, 1989.

Crichton, M. *Travels*. New York: Knopf, 1988.

Dossey, L. *Space, Time, and Medicine*. Boston: New Science Library, 1982.

Drury, N. *The Shaman and the Magician: Journeys between the Worlds*. London: Arkana, 1982.

Eisler, R. *The Chalice and the Blade: Our History, Our Future*. San Francisco: Harper San Francisco, 1988.

Eliade, M. *Shamanism: Archaic Techniques of Ecstasy*. London: Arkana, 1989.

Epstein, G. *Healing Visualizations: Creating Health through Imagery*. New York: Bantam Books, 1989.

Fisher, R. "A cartography of the ecstatic and meditative states." *Science* 174 (1971): 897–904.

Garfield, P. *Creative Dreaming*. New York: Ballantine Books, 1974.

Gartelmann, K. *Digging Up Prehistory: The Archeology of Ecuador*. Quito, Ecuador: Ediciones Libri Mundi, 1986.

Harner, M. *The Jivaro: People of the Sacred Waterfalls*. Berkeley and Los Angeles: University of California Press, 1984.

Harrison, R. *Signs, Songs, and Memory in the Andes: Translating Quechua Language and Culture*. Austin: University of Texas Press, 1989.

Jacobson, E. *Progressive Relaxation*. Chicago: University of Chicago Press, 1938.

James, E. *Attaining the Mastership: Advanced Studies on the Spiritual Path*. Atlanta: Dhamma Books, 1988.

Jana, H. "Energy metabolsim in hypnotic trance and sleep." *Journal of Applied Physiology* 20 (1965): 308–10.

Jung, C. *Memories, Dreams, Reflections*. New York: Vintage Books, 1961.

Kalweit, H. *Dreamtime and Inner Space: The World of the Shaman*. Boston: Shambhala, 1988.

Katkin, H. S., and E. N. Murray. "Instrumental conditioning of automatically mediated behavior: Theoretical and methodological issues." *Psychological Bulletin* 70 (1968): 52–68.

King, S. K. *Urban Shaman*. New York: Fireside, 1990.

Kühlewind, G. *Stages of Consciousness: Meditations on the Boundaries of the Soul*. Stockbridge, Mass.: Inner Traditions/Lindisfarne Press, 1984.

Lamb, B. F. *Wizard of the Upper Amazon*. Berkeley, Calif.: North Atlantic Books, 1974.

Lame Deer, J. Fire, and R. Erdoes. *Lame Deer: Seeker of Visions*. New York: Simon and Schuster, 1972. Reprint. London: Quartet, 1980.

Laszlo, E. *Introduction to Systems Philosophy: Toward a New Paradigm of Contemporary Thought*. Foreword by Ludwig von Bertalanffy. New York: Harper Torchbooks, 1973.

Lawlor, R. *Earth Honoring: The New Male Sexuality*. Rochester, Vt.: Park Street Press, 1989.

————. *Voices of the First Day: Awakening in the Aboriginal Dreamtime.* Rochester, Vt.: Inner Traditions, 1991.

Lidell, L., N. Rabinovitch, and G. Rabinovitch. *The Sivananda Companion to Yoga.* New York: Simon and Schuster, 1983.

Lovelock, J. E. *Gaia: A New Look at Life on Earth.* Oxford: Oxford University Press, 1987.

Luthe, W. ed. *Autogenic Therapy,* vols. 1–5. New York: Grune and Stratton, 1969.

Mander, J. *In the Absence of the Sacred: The Failure of Technology and the Survival of the Indian Nations.* San Francisco: Sierra Club Books, 1991.

McIntyre, L. *The Incredible Incas and Their Timeless Land.* Washington, D.C.: National Geographic Society, 1975.

McKenna, T. *The Archaic Revival: Speculations on Psychedelic Mushrooms, the Amazon, Virtual Reality, UFOs, Evolution, Shamanism, the Birth of the Goddess, and the End of History.* San Francisco: Harper San Francisco, 1991.

Melville, A. *With Eyes to See: A Journey from Religion to Spirituality.* Walpole, N.H.: Stillpoint, 1992.

Monroe, R. *Journeys out of the Body.* New York: Doubleday, 1971.

Moss, G. E. *Illness, Immunity, and Social Interaction: The Dynamics of Biosocial Resonation.* New York: 1973.

Naranjo, C., and R. E. Ornstein. *On the Psychology of Meditation.* New York: Viking Press, 1971.

Organ, T. W. *The Hindu Quest for the Perfection of Man.* Athens, Ohio: Ohio University Press, 1970.

Ornstein, R. E. *The Psychology of Consciousness.* San Francisco: Freeman, 1972.

Perkins, J. *Psychonavigation: Techniques for Travel beyond Time.* Rochester, Vt.: Destiny Books, 1990.

————. *The Stress-Free Habit: Powerful Techniques for Health and Longevity from the Andes, Yucatan, and Far East.* Rochester, Vt.: Healing Arts Press, 1989.

Pilkington, R. "Cyberphysiology in children." *Advances: Journal of the Institute for the Advancement of Health 5,* no. 4 (1988): 66–69.

Popescu, P. *Amazon Beaming.* New York: Viking Press, 1991.

Rodríguez, G. *La faz occulta de la medicina andina.* Quito, Ecuador: Núcleo de América Ecuatorial, 1992.

Schultes, R. E., and R. F. Raffauf. *Vine of the Soul: Medicine Men, Their Plants and Rituals in the Colombian Amazonia.* Oracle, Ariz.: Synergetic Press, 1992.

Sheldrake, R. *A New Science of Life: the Hypothesis of Formative Causation.* Los Angeles: Tarcher, 1987.

Singh, D. *Spiritual Awakening.* Bowling Green, Va.: Sawan Kirpa, 1986.

Slocum, J. *Sailing Alone around the World.* New York: Dover, 1956.

Spaulding, B. *Life and Teachings of the Masters of the Far East,* vols. 1–3. Marina Del Rey, Calif.: DeVorss, 1944.

Stevens, J., and L. S. Stevens. *Secrets of Shamanism: Tapping the Spirit Power within You.* New York: Avon Books, 1988.

Swimme, B., and T. Berry. *The Universe Story: From the Primordial Flaring Forth to the Ecozoic Era: A Celebration of the Unfolding of the Cosmos.* San Francisco: Harper San Francisco, 1992.

Triminham, J. S. *Sufi Orders in Islam.* Oxford: Clarendon Press, 1971.

Van Hagen, V. *The Ancient Sun Kingdoms of the Americas.* London: Thames and Hudson, 1962.

Villoldo, A., and S. Krippner. *Healing States: A Journey into the World of Spiritual Healing and Shamanism.* New York: Simon and Schuster, 1987.

Wakefield, C. *High Cities of the Andes.* San Carlos, Calif.: Wide World/ Tetra, 1988.

Wallace, R. K. "Physiological effects of transcendental meditation." *Science* 167 (1970): 1751–54.

Wallace, R. K., and H. Benson. "The physiology of meditation." *Scientific American* 226 (1972): 84–90.

Weiss, B. L. *Many Lives, Many Masters.* New York: Fireside, 1988.

———. *Through Time into Healing.* New York: Fireside, 1992.

Wolf, F. A. *The Eagle's Quest: A Physicist's Search for Truth in the Heart of the Shamanic World.* New York: Summit Books, 1991.

Wood, C. Herpes: Think positive. *Psychology Today* (December 1986), 24.

———. Relaxation really works. *Psychology Today* (January 1987), 68.

Zukav, G. *The Seat of the Soul.* New York: Fireside, 1990.

Earth Dream Alliance is a nonprofit organization established by people who have participated in trips led by John Perkins to the Ecuadoran shamans. EDA is dedicated to inspiring Earth-honoring changes in consciousness, preserving forests, and applying indigenous wisdom in ways that foster environmental and social balance.

A primary EDA objective is to purchase and conserve large areas of forest in the Amazon and Andes on behalf of the indigenous people and to help these people establish shamanic learning centers, where they can exchange information with one another as well as with visitors from other parts of the world. EDA sponsors workshops, programs for students, and other forums where people learn to empower the subconscious and create new ways of dreaming the world, where alliances are formed and wisdom is exchanged. Many of EDA's workshops are conducted by John Perkins in Ecuador and are combined with trips to visit and work with the shamans described in *The World Is As You Dream It.*

For information about EDA trips and workshops, please contact: Earth Dream Alliance, P.O. Box 2219, Jupiter, FL 33468, (407) 744-7600. If you have any comments or questions for the author, please write to:

John Perkins
c/o Prydwen
P.O. Box 31357
Palm Beach Gardens, FL 33420